For Judith A. Schiff
with gratitude for her
kindness

sincerely,

Albert Shumate

George Gordon's California

GEORGE GORDON
Born in London, England, 1818, as George Cummings.
Courtesy of Stanford University Archives.

THE CALIFORNIA OF GEORGE GORDON

and the 1849 sea voyages of his California Association

a San Francisco pioneer
rescued from the legend
of Gertrude Atherton's first novel

by
ALBERT SHUMATE

with Foreword by
RICHARD H. DILLON

THE ARTHUR H. CLARK COMPANY
Glendale, California
1976

Contents

Illustrations

In Preface and Acknowledgment

A number of years ago, George Harding, then the head of the lusty San Francisco chapter of E Clampus Vitus, suggested I write an article about South Park and Rincon Hill as the Clampers were soon to visit that early residential area of San Francisco. This led to my 1963 booklet, "A Visit to Rincon Hill and South Park." The end result was that I found myself intrigued with Gertrude Atherton's lurid story about George Gordon, the developer of South Park. Could it be fact, or was it fiction?

During the years which have followed, I have immersed myself in an enjoyable search for the truth behind the Gordon legend, a search that has led to England, Nicaragua, Colorado, New Mexico, and California as well as the East Coast of the United States. Over the years, I have been aided by many; in fact, the kindness of all concerned has been overwhelming.

First I would like to thank Ruth Teiser for her assistance in the writing of this biography. I am also greatly indebted to Richard H. Dillon for his Foreword. I also received enormous aid from L. C. Suggars in England who solved many of the mysteries surrounding Gordon's origins. I am also deeply indebted to my former secretary Margaret Jungsten and to Mrs. Bland Platt for the time they devoted to this manuscript. And I wish to extend special appreciation to Mr. and Mrs. Everett G. Hager for compiling the book's index. Special thanks, too, to Frances Hoxie of the Connecticut Historical

Society for providing contemporary accounts of the
voyage of the *Clarissa Perkins,* and to Judith A. Schiff
at the Yale University Library for giving me permission to use the Baldwin Family Papers as well as the
papers of Samuel Smith Woods and Charles Thompson
Blake.

I would also like to thank the following who pro-
vided the necessary information regarding the later life
of Doctor C. C. Gordon: Brinley MacLaren of the
Denver Medical Society Library; Alice Sharp of the
Historical Society of Colorado; Wesley Draper, librar-
ian of the Academy of Medicine of Brooklyn, New
York; and especially S. Omar Barker of Las Vegas,
New Mexico.

I am also greatly indebted to the following historical
societies and libraries for assisting me in ferreting out
the obvious as well as the obscure from their collections:
James Abajian, Mrs. M. K. Swingle, Lee Burtis, Jay
Williar and Terry Mangan of the California Historical Society; Robert Becker and staff at the Bancroft
Library; Dr. Ray Billington of the Huntington Library; Ethel S. Crockett, Allan Ottley and Therese
Lawrence at the State Library in Sacramento; Elliot
Evans and his staff at the Society of California Pioneers; Harold Elliott and staff at the Federal Archives
in San Bruno; Wilbur Smith and Brooke Whiting in
the Special Collections Department of the UCLA
Library; and the staffs of the Sutro Library, the San
Francisco Maritime Museum, the Mechanics Institute,
and the California Academy of Sciences Library.

Further assistance was provided by Ralph Hansen
at the Stanford University Library; Dr. William Davis
at the State Archives; Barbara Barton, Bank of California Library; Irene Neasham and the staff at the

Wells Fargo History Room; Gladys Hansen who heads the Rare Books and Special Collections Room at the San Francisco Public Library; Karl Vollmayer of the Redwood City Public Library; the Rev. William Monihan, S.J., and Florian Shasky of the University of San Francisco Library, and particularly Catherine Harroun.

Others who have given unstintingly of their valuable time and assistance include: Clyde Arbuckle; Newt Baird; Gunther Barth; Ray Bloss; Barron B. Beshoar (Colorado); Dr. Phyllis Bentley (England); Sister M. Colette, O.P., of Dominican College; Ann Campbell; Carlo DeFerrari; Ferrol Egan; Walter Frame; John B. Goodman, III; Warren Howell; Mrs. George Harding; Miss Catherine Hoover; Gardiner Johnson; Helen Kuezel; Mrs. Philip F. Landis; Mrs. Lloyd Luckmann; Oscar Lewis; Frank Maher; Ed Mannion; Merrill J. Mattes; Kendrick Miller; Doyce Nunis; Maria Eleana Ossa; Helen van Cleve Park; Mrs. David Potter; Anne Petterson (New York); Rodman Paul; Joan Quigley; Dorothy Regnery; Millie Robbins; Gordon Roskilly (Saint Andrews Society); Constance Sevier; Joseph William Smith; Louis Stein; Mrs. George Thacher; Jeffrey Thomas; Suzanne Wellborn; and Dr. R. Coke Wood.

Finally my thanks to Keith Wedmore, Chairman of the Board of Mawer and Collingham, Ltd., Lincoln, England; Mrs. Charles B. Howland and Luella Swergert in Pennsylvania; and the late Dwight L. Clarke, Emerson Greenaway, John A. Hawgood, and Thomas W. Streeter.

ALBERT SHUMATE

Foreword

by RICHARD H. DILLON

San Francisco – like Rome – was not built in a day, although it is America's most instantaneous of cities. In the frenetic pace of its early growth, it makes such Western boomtowns as Denver seem almost sedate.

Nor was the building of San Francisco the work of one man, the biographers of William C. Ralston notwithstanding. Proof positive of this claim lies within the pages of this excellent life of George Gordon. If the latter is remembered at all today in the City, it is as the creator of elegant South Park, the West's first planned urban development. But this fair copy of Gramercy Park in New York, or London's Holland Park, was but one of many contributions to the early history of San Francisco made by the enigmatic Gordon.

The biographer of this mystery man belongs to that rare breed of historians which, we trust, is not an endangered species. Dr. Albert Shumate is neither a professor, like Gunther Barth or Walton Bean, nor a freelance professional of history, like Oscar Lewis or David Lavender. And he is certainly not a mere run-of-the-book-stacks antiquarian. No, the author is an amateur of history in the old sense, in the best sense of the word. In recent years, through constant misuse, the word *amateur* has been debased in America. It is now carelessly treated as a synonym for dilettante, meaning a trifler or dabbler in some field or other. But the true amateur is a lover of the subject matter of his avocation, as suggested by the original meaning of this word, borrowed from the French. But more; the gifted amateur of history, like Dr. Shumate, is quite as accomplished, as expert, in his avocation as he is in his profession or calling, if not more so.

Thus, Dr. Shumate resembles his contemporary, Kenneth Johnson of the legal profession, and such a predecessor from his own field of medicine as the late Dr. George D. Lyman, author of *John Marsh, Pioneer* and *Ralston's Ring*. What is most striking about the men and women of this ilk is not their general thoroughness of research or the care and polish of their exposition. It is their sheer inquisitiveness! They are as close to Sherlock and Mycroft Holmes as they are to John and Theodore H. Hittell.

Dr. Shumate's dogged detective work, carried out over many years and thousands of miles of geography, from San Francisco to Middlesex, has succeeded where that of several so-called professionals has failed. He has penetrated his biographee's deliberate secrecy about his early life just as he has cut his way through the legend, myth and fiction written about Gordon by a number of popular authors of San Francisco history. The name always used in America by the subject of this biography, George Gordon, was not his real name. The age given in obituaries and on his very tombstone was incorrect. Certainly he was never "Lord" Gordon, as some writers would have it.

Very carefully, the author has contrasted documented fact with the historical fiction of Gertrude Atherton's *romans a clef* which were supposedly "based" on the Gordon family saga. He has found that the novelist detonated a small grain of truth into a shock wave of sensationalist fiction which titillated and scandalized polite society by the Golden Gate. Her two books, *The Randolphs of Redwoods* and *A Daughter of the Vine* are important in our literary history as precursors of the realism of Frank Norris and others. But as history or biography the value of the two lurid shockers is worse than nil. Unfortunately, they inspired a series of articles and book-chapters which pretended to be nonfiction but which were composed of equal parts of fiction and wild surmise. (Perhaps it is not too late for Gertrude Atherton to have her poetic license revoked, posthumously, for altering San Francisco history.)

Even Dr. Shumate cannot explain why Gordon changed his name before coming to America, any more than California historians have been able to explain why Grizzly Adams took his brother's name, instead of his own, when he westered to the Sierra Nevada. The doctor's suggestion that Gordon, then a tea importer in England, might have strayed into smuggling, is not just "as good a guess as any." It is something more than that. Violation of the revenue laws of Great Britain might very well initiate emigration and a change of name. But it was not so heinous a crime that Gordon could not "surface" in San Francisco society without a morbid fear of being recognized and exposed as George Cummings of Middlesex, tea smuggler. In short, it is a very likely possibility.

Our biographer successfully peels away onion-like layers of legend, too, in order to reveal the historical core of the Gordon story. He demolishes the wild tales – that Gordon's wife was an ex-barmaid; that she hated him; that she punished him by dosing their daughter's milk with whiskey and turned her into a precocious lush. Dr. Shumate concludes, partially from the medical evidence relating to her death, that Mrs. Gordon

did, indeed, have a drinking problem. And her brother
was a prodigious tippler. But not all of the actors in the
drama were alcoholics; certainly not Gordon himself.
If he drank heavily, he knew how to hold it.

Some readers will regret that Dr. Shumate, in re-
searching and writing the definitive account of George
Gordon, has, alas, expertly destroyed more than one
humdinger of a yarn.

In this book he follows Gordon from his shadowy
beginnings in England to his sad death. Gordon first
came to notice in an all-too-typical Gold Rush adven-
ture. Like so many men of drive and imagination in
1849, he finagled the captaincy of an emigrant party by
dint of considerable bluffing, promises, and advertising.
Like Lansford Hastings, he was entrepreneur, speculator, promoter, spellbinder and, just possibly, a bit of a
flim-flam man. His company made it safely to El
Dorado, all right, but hardly with the ease and dispatch
predicted by their leader.

To Gordon's great credit, however, he veered off
toward the straight and narrow path once he was in
California. He became as productive and honest a San
Francisco businessman as we are likely to find in
that catch-as-catch-can era, when terms like "business
ethics" and "conflict of interest" had not yet begun to
ring in the corridors of commerce. He was not interested in metamorphosing from captain of industry into
robber baron, *a la* Sharon and Huntington. Certainly,
he never betrayed his friends for cash, as did lumber-
man Honest Harry Meiggs, Wells Fargo's absconding
Charley Banks, or expressman I. C. Woods, all of
whom lit out from the Embarcadero by ship, just one
jump ahead of John Law.

For the first time, we see in this volume the full

accomplishments of a major figure in early Bay Area business and industry. Gordon ranks with the likes of Brannan, Ralston and Sutro as a mover and a doer. He ran a few board feet of Nicaraguan lumber into a fortune, a country estate, and control of the Vulcan Iron Works and the San Francisco and Pacific Sugar Refinery, among other enterprises. He enjoyed a colorful and important career, if not a long one.

Gordon, like his biographer, was accomplished in his avocation. He was a public-spirited pamphleteer and an inveterate writer of letters-to-the-editor. Perhaps the latter habit was a throwback to his days of perusing the *Times* in the Home Counties. He wrote well on such serious and important topics as the earthquake-proofing of buildings. In lobbying for safety at sea, he became a sort of Samuel Plimsoll of San Francisco. He was not afraid to take the unpopular side in public controversies. Though he never became a citizen, he opposed the violence of the Vigilance Committee of 1856 because of his patriotic zeal for American institutions and democracy, for law and order. He wrote that the Vigilantes had "violated the sacred compacts and guarantees of the Constitution of the United States for the sake of remedying local evils. . ." and "subverted recognized law under the plea of administering substantial justice." When warhawkish partisans of both North and South pulled and tugged at him in 1861, he stolidly stood his ground and urged peace and compromise – *anything* (even two separate countries) rather than a bloody civil war.

So patriotic was Gordon that he offended many Scots when he addressed the St. Andrews Society and compared Caledonia, unfavorably, to California.

George Gordon worked in behalf of immigration,

hospitals, the YMCA, the Chamber of Commerce, and the Art Institute. At his death, newspaper obituaries saluted him, properly, as a man who had understood the relationship between personal success and the success of the community in which he lived.

Gordon's rise had not been slow but his fall, and that of his family, was incredibly fast. With his death, his family literally fell apart – as if under a curse (perhaps the curse of drink). He refused to attend his daughter's wedding because he detested her husband-to-be. He then grieved over this seeming betrayal by Nellie, always the apple of his eye, till his health was ruined. No doctor could put the correct cause on his death certificate, of course, but he died of a broken heart only three months after the ceremony. In a deathbed codicil he cut his daughter out of his will.

By 1872, Nellie and her husband were separated. Their only child had died in infancy. In 1874, Nellie, only 29, died and her mother followed her to the grave in just two months. It took Gordon's dissolute brother-in-law a little longer, but he drank himself to death by '76, and his wife continued the downward spiral. She was an ex-housemaid of the Gordons, described as never having drawn a sober breath.

Drunkenness was probably always present in the family. But it became rampant when death removed the man who alone could hold the alcoholic edifice of Mayfield Estate together. The Gordon family then destroyed itself.

Bret Harte in 1864 wrote a poem about George Gordon which he titled "South Park." It is waggish doggerel, to be sure, but there is more truth than poesy in one stanza, wherein he observes that George Gordon was a man "of private fortune, and of public worth."

The California of
George Gordon

Gertrude Atherton
and the Gordon Legend

The Gordon Legend, like the legends of Joaquin Murietta and Concepción Argüello, has long fascinated those with an interest in the lore of California. However, few realize that Gertrude Atherton, one of California's best known authors, is responsible for creating and introducing, and later reinterpreting and magnifying the sensational aspects of the rise and fall of the House of Gordon.

Gertrude Horn Atherton was born in 1857 in San Francisco's fashionable Rincon Hill district. Her mother was the daughter of Stephen Franklin, a highly respected banker, and her father was Thomas L. Horn, a wealthy business man whose brother, Benjamin Horn, also lived on Rincon Hill in a Gothic mansion that was long a landmark. Since the Horn residence was located only a block from the Gordon family's South Park home, one may presume the Horns knew and visited the Gordons. Gertrude's parents' marriage lasted only three years, ending in divorce, as did her mother's second marriage to John F. Uhlhorn, scion of an old New York family.

In 1875, when young Gertrude returned to California from a year of schooling at the Sayre Institute in Lexington, Kentucky, she found George Atherton courting her mother, who was fourteen years young Atherton's senior. George was the son of Faxon Dean Atherton, one of the leading financiers of the Pacific

Coast, and Dominga de Goni Atherton, a member of an aristocratic Chilean family. A strict Catholic, Mrs. Atherton viewed her son's romance with a divorced woman with intense displeasure. To everyone's astonishment, however, it was the nineteen year old Gertrude who eloped with George Atherton on February 14, 1876. Needless to say, Gertrude's mother was less than pleased, to put it mildly, while George's mother was conspicuously upset.

"When I heard of the marriage of George I felt so drawn to you that I could hardly keep from writing to you of my sympathy and love to you all," wrote Mrs. Thomas H. Selby, Mrs. Faxon Atherton's neighbor and the wife of the San Francisco industrialist and former mayor. Mrs. Selby continued: "My dear friend, none of us ought to depend upon our children for our happiness." But Mrs. Selby did concede that: "He has married a young and pretty girl."

Years later, Gertrude Atherton wrote in her autobiography, *Adventures of a Novelist,* that the Athertons "did not receive me with open arms, for no less demonstrative people ever lived, but they were philosophical and they had escaped a great calamity" – George's marriage to a divorcee.

Gertrude's marriage to George was, alas for romance, not successful. She was bored and later wrote of Valparaiso Park, the Atherton home in Menlo Park: "I hated everyone in it, George most of all." Still later, she belittled her marriage as "one of the most important incidents of my school life." She read extensively and nourished a great desire to write. Many years later, she explained: "I was born to be a writer and nothing else, unendowed by high heaven with either the maternal or domestic instincts."

Mrs. Faxon Atherton reacted to her daughter-in-law's idea of becoming a writer in a very definite manner: "Ladies in Spain do not write." This was not just the opinion of one fashionable lady. Amelia Ransome Neville, who knew not only San Francisco but international society, wrote in her charming book *Fantastic City* that "young ladies were not encouraged to be bookish" and again, "Reading was not fashionable in the eighteen fifties," that being the period when Mrs. Faxon Atherton was a young matron.

Then, one memorable morning, the bored Gertrude read a newspaper article which was to change her life. To quote again from her autobiography: "But one day I had nothing to read . . . a copy of the morning newspaper lay on the floor . . . my eye was caught by a familiar name, Nelly Gordon. ("Nellie" was the spelling used by the Gordon family.) The story . . . enthralled me . . . before I had finished, it seemed to me that something was battering at a sealed door in my brain. . . Here was a story at last and I would write it."

The article was in the San Francisco *Morning Call* of November 18, 1882. It read as follows:

WHAT AM I BID?
AN AUCTION SALE OF FUNERAL AND WEDDING TRAPPINGS
"What am I offered?"
"Oh, don't sell that," said one or two bidders.
The auctioneer held up a large walnut case. It contained a funeral wreath of preserved flowers.
"Well, I've sold coffins at auction in my time; so I guess I can stand this," replied the auctioneer. "What am I offered?"
He disposed of it, with three other funeral mementoes, very cheap, for the bidding was dispirited.
It was at the sale yesterday, in a Montgomery Street auction room, of the personal effects, jewelry, silverware and household bric-a-brac of a once very wealthy San Francisco family. The

head of the family was a pioneer, a citizen of wealth, and high social and commercial standing. It was he, who in early days, projected the South Park.

There was no family in the city whose society was more sought after, or who entertained better than George Gordon.

"What am I offered for this lot?"

He referred to the lot catalogued as "No. 107," and described as "Wedding dress, shoes, etc."

"Don't sell that!" The very old clo' man remonstrated this time.

It seemed worse than the sale of the funeral wreath. This was all that remained to remind the old citizens present of one of the happiest events in the history of the well-known family. The dress was heavy with white satin – had been, that is; it was yellowed with time. The tiny shoes had evidently been worn but once.

"What am I offered? Make a bid, gentlemen. I offer the lot. What am I offered?"

"One dollar!"

"One dollar I am offered for the lot – wedding dress, shoes, etc. One dollar for the lot. Come, gentlemen, bid up."

Not an old clo' man in the room bid, and the outsider who bid the one dollar had the happiness to see it knocked down to him.

"What am I bid for this photograph album. Bid up, gentlemen. Here's a chance to get at the collection of photographs of distinguished citizens, their wives and daughters."

A gentleman quietly standing on the edge of the crowd bid on the album. When it was handed to him he opened it, took out his own and the photographs of several well dressed ladies, dressed in the fashion of twenty years ago, some of them, and then tossed the album, with the other photographs in a stove, remarking: "Well, they won't go to the junk shop."

"What am I offered, gentlemen, for this? There is just seventeen dollars worth of gold in it. Bid up."

The auctioneer held up and exhibited an engraved gold medal. It was a Crimean war medal, which its owner was once proud to wear. There was a time in his life when no money could have purchased it. He had risked his life in one of the Highland regiments for the honor of wearing it, and after his death it was offered for gold.

"Twenty dollars!"

"Twenty dollars; twenty, twenty, twenty; Mind your bid, gentlemen. Seventeen dollars for the gold and three for the honor. Twenty, tw-en-ty and going, going, gone! Seventeen dollars for the gold and three for the honor!"

In this way an ebony writing desk, with the dead citizen's private letters, was sold to a hand-me-down shop keeper; a tin box with private papers went to a junk dealer, and different lots of classical music, some worn, some marked with givers' names, some with verses written on the pages, were sold to the second-hand dealers. "What am I bid?" The sale went rapidly on. Sometimes an old family friend would bid an article as a souvenir, a champagne cooler, a salad dish, silver tongs, etc. But the junk dealers, second-hand men and hand-me-down shop keepers took in most of the goods.

This article was the first of many to circulate inaccuracies about the Gordon family. Specifically, Gordon had been in San Francisco during the Crimean War and, therefore, had won no battlefield medals there or anywhere else! But the article had stimulated Gertrude Atherton's imagination, and she determined to write a novel based on the tragic story of the Gordon family.

It must be remembered that excellent sources of information were available to her. The 1882 auction sale took place only fourteen years after George Gordon's death, nine years after his wife and daughter had died, and four years after the death of the last of his heirs. Then, too, as a child, Gertrude Atherton had overheard her mother and her mother's friends discussing the Gordons. In 1932, she wrote in *Adventures of a Novelist:* "I was all ears and overheard much gossip when I was supposed to be reading fairy tales in a corner of the large front bedroom and my mother was enjoying an afternoon visit from her more intimate friends. Of course, the talk was all dress, personalities and scandals." One scandal was, of course, that of the Gordons and of ". . . Nelly Gordon, whose father had built

South Park. Even then there were rumors that she 'drank', and her terrible old mother, never seen, was supposed to be in a perpetual state of inebriety."

Gertrude had later learned more about the Gordons from the Athertons, particularly from her husband, and his sister Alejandra. According to a contemporary letter written by Prentis Selby, George Atherton and his sisters had ridden horseback with Nellie Gordon during their teens, for the Athertons' Menlo Park home was near Mayfield Grange, the Gordons' estate located just south of San Francisquito Creek.

Gertrude also gleaned a certain amount of information from the Gordons' attorney, John T. Doyle, who was a Menlo Park neighbor of both the Athertons and the Gordons and who had loaned her books in hopes of relieving her boredom.

Probably no other person had had as much influence upon the Gordons as did John Thomas Doyle. A leading California attorney, he had arrived in San Francisco in 1851. While the legal cases in which he was involved were some of the most important in California, he is best known for his work in the Pious Fund case. The Pious Fund was established in the seventeenth century to provide revenue for the missions of California. However, after Mexico obtained its independence from Spain, the Fund was gradually absorbed by the Mexican government. With Upper California becoming part of the United States in 1848, California church authorities attempted to obtain the money owed them. In 1853, Bishop Alemany of San Francisco sought Doyle's counsel, and until his death in 1906, Doyle was involved in this lengthy suit, which was not finally settled until 1967.

Doyle is also remembered for his service as President

of the California Historical Society during its earliest years and as a member of the Board of Regents of the University of California. Four years before his death, he wrote a memoir about his friend and client George Gordon. Located at Stanford University, this narrative, unfortunately containing little that is accurate regarding Gordon's early years, principally retells the story of Gordon's expedition to California.

Although Gertrude's sources of information may have been excellent, the novel she subsequently wrote was far from an accurate account of the history of the Gordon family as we shall later see. She entitled this, her first novel, *The Randolphs of Redwoods* and submitted it to the editors of a leading San Francisco weekly, the *Argonaut*. To her great delight, they decided to publish it.

Because of the prominent San Francisco social personages depicted in the novel – not only the Gordons, but also Mrs. Hall McAllister, the "three Macs" (well known belles Mollie McMullin, Ella Maxwell, and Jennie McNulty), the Leander Ransomes, the Athertons, the Barrons of the New Almaden mines and possibly a brother of John T. Doyle – the editors advised that the novel be published anonymously. Although the novelist had disguised the names, the social world of San Francisco was small and the characters were readily identifiable.

Frank Pixley, the *Argonaut's* editor-in-chief, predicted the story would create a sensation, and it certainly did! The first installment appeared in the March 31, 1883, issue and was followed by five more in succeeding weeks. Public reaction was reflected in letters to the editors in which the novel was branded as "immoral" and "infamous." To quote from a letter printed in the issue of April 14, 1883:

To the Editor of the Argonaut:

While you are straightening out all the crooked things on this planet and adjacent ones, would it not be well for you to pay more attention to editing your valuable and instructive journal.

The serial now running would be exceedingly interesting to readers of the Police Gazette, but hardly to be placed in the hands of the youth of the City.

Another letter, dated April 30, 1883, which appeared in the May 5th issue, reads in part:

. . . its reproduction of a family and its sad vices, giving in every paragraph earmarks by which recognition is immediate and painful, is to say the very least, both indelicate and offensive. People had quite forgotten the mournful history and why galvanize it in a form so distorted? . . . Believe me, that little drama now reaching its catastrophe in your paper – in which appears not only the truth, but in addition much misstatement – violates all the proprieties.

The editor responded:

It contains a healthful moral . . . It is a temperance lecture to a class which does not often enough consider the terrible effects of a pernicious habit. . . that thoughtless mothers shall, after reading it, guard with more watchful vigilance their daughters as they go out into the giddy whirl of society. . .

He declared in conclusion that the *Randolphs* had "a moral which it is better to heed than to carp at."

Two letters indicate that rumors of the Gordon family's alcoholic tendencies were common knowledge at the time:

To the Editor (San Francisco *News Letter,* April 21, 1883):

. . . There dwelt in Frisco a family of three, who entertained hospitably, and were people of position and wealth. The two ladies of the family had a besetting sin; everyone knew and knows of it – but – all three being dead and buried, in the name of common decency – common humanity – why not let their faults and miseries be buried with them?

This same letter stigmatizes the serial as the "French-iest of the French." The other letter (to the *Argonaut*) states:

> I recognize in this narrative, *The Randolphs of Redwoods,* the painful and shameful story of a family which once lived in this city, a family which was rich and prosperous, a family which is extinct today. And ruin, shame and death brought upon this family was caused by DRINK.

These are merely examples of the furor to which *The Randolphs of Redwoods* gave rise on its publication.

A columnist in the *Argonaut* then commented on the mystery of who wrote the serial: "If it be a man people will shun him, if it be a woman, poor thing, she will be formally drummed out of Society to the clack of the indignant dowager's tongue and the fife of the shrill-voiced rosebud."

But, as Gertrude Atherton noted, Society was not her milieu. She was content to devote herself instead to becoming one of the most prolific and widely read of American authors.

Writing in *The Bookman* of February 1931, Charles Caldwell Dobie assessed the literary significance of *The Randolphs of Redwoods:* "It was a sordid story without any outstanding literary merit save one – a ruthless candor. Anything approaching truth in fiction was a new idea to a community wallowing in romantic complacency. . . It is the work of a novice not yet trained in her art. But its value lies in the fact that it was the first realistic novel to come out of the Pacific Coast."

Typical of her style in that early work is the following from the first installment of her story. The Randolphs (the Gordons) are giving a ball in their South Park home; Nina (Nellie) is talking to Colonel St. John in the conservatory:

. . . Suddenly, in reply to some audacious remark on my part
— attributable to the champagne — she struck me a light blow with
her fan, and sprang to her feet. As she did so she staggered
slightly, and, as a matter of course, I caught her. She made no
effort to release herself, and I gathered her comfortably in and
looked down upon her, while she returned my gaze with interest.
She was leaning with all her weight against me, and in a position
which the word "abandon" doth poorly express. Between the
scarlet outline of her dress and the dark blue of my coat her ivory
neck and shoulders gleamed more alluringly than ever, and her
hair, slightly ruffled, lent an additional softness to her piquant,
flushed face.

Not being a saint, I made no attempt to resist. In short, I kissed
her. Meeting no rebuke, I repeated the operation not once, but
many times, and ended finally by kissing every available inch of
her anatomy bared to public view. Her skin was like satin in tex-
ture, but for firmness and warmth could be compared to nothing
short of the divine, and I was about to go back to the beginning
and go through the entire performance a second time, when, suddenly, before I could realize her intention, she twisted herself out
of my arms, darted down the conservatory, and up the stairs on
the opposite side of the hall. We remained until a late hour, but
I saw her no more that night.

"Hilton," I said, as we drove out toward Fort Point in the
dawn, "what kind of a girl is Miss Randolph?"

The novel follows the Gordon story with some ac-
curacy — the alcoholic tendencies of Mrs. Gordon and
probably her daughter's, the sites of their city and country residences, the meeting with the ship's doctor who
in time became Nellie's husband, George Gordon's
grief concerning this marriage, and the arrival of Mrs.
Gordon's brother, his subsequent marriage to the servant girl, and his alcoholism. However, the incident of
an ill-fated love affair between Nellie and an Army
officer resulting in a child born out of wedlock is extremely doubtful. And the assertion that Nellie was
taken to Europe by her father to escape her mother's

evil influence is completely untrue as will be seen later.

When the Atherton family learned that Gertrude had written the sensational serial, they were not pleased; no doubt, they were even less pleased by her nom de plume, "Asmodeus," the evil Hebrew demon of matrimonial unhappiness!

Joseph Henry Jackson, writing in the San Francisco *Chronicle,* November 1, 1942, summed up the turmoil: "In those days nice young women just didn't write. . . For a time Gertrude Atherton was cold shouldered by everyone who knew that she had done something so wicked, improper, cynical, scandalous and altogether abominable as to write *The Randolphs of Redwoods."*

But Gertrude Atherton continued to write, not only newspaper and magazine serials, but full-fledged novels as well. And she continued to be severely criticized. For example, in 1889, one critic, in reviewing her early book *Hermia Suydam,* wrote: "Her methods – if methods they are – are somewhat illogical; in other words, feminine." While obviously critical of Mrs. Atherton's style, the reviewer could not resist the opportunity to ridicule a woman's having the audacity to write professionally. Then, too, Mrs. Atherton consistently selected subject matter that was considered sensational and hardly appropriate for a lady. Louisa May Alcott's *Little Women* or Frances Hodgson Burnett's *Little Lord Fauntleroy,* on the other hand, were more palatable to the masculine mind, which had not as yet accepted women as serious writers.

In the 1890s, while living in Haworth, England, Gertrude Atherton rewrote *The Randolphs of Redwoods,* this time entitling it *A Daughter of the Vine.* In her autobiography, she recalled: "It had seemed to me that Haworth was the place to rewrite *The Randolphs* for Nelly Gordon's parents had lived in Yorkshire, and *possibly her father* [italics are mine] had known Branwell Bronte and caroused with him in the bar-parlor of the Black Bull Inn. I had hoped to hear legends of the Gordons but oldsters had no memories of any part of Yorkshire but their immediate corner of it. I knew that Mr. Gordon had been one of the wild bloods of the country and on a drunken spree had married the barmaid who was to curse his life and Nelly's. . . She was the cause of his immigration to California."

A Daughter of the Vine is a much better novel than the crude *The Randolphs of Redwoods,* but it is an even less accurate account of the Gordons.

In the new version, the hero is a visiting Englishman (a character Mrs. Atherton used in several of her stories). Like the Army officer in *The Randolphs,* he becomes the father of Nina's child, born out of wedlock. In this novel, Nina (Nellie) gives an account of her family background: her father belonged to one of the oldest families in the country, residing in Keighly, her mother was a barmaid at the Lord Rodney Inn at Keighly, and her father was a drinking companion of Branwell Bronte, the dissipated brother of the famous Bronte sisters. According to Nina, Randolph (Gordon) awoke after a prolonged spree to find himself married to the barmaid. Disgraced, he traveled to the little town of Yerba Buena. (As a matter of fact, the village's name had been changed to San Francisco two years before Gordon arrived in 1849.) Nina further states that Randolph owned a ranch in Lake County and had had a distinguished career in the Crimean War, neither of which Gordon did. And most sensational of all, Ger-

GERTRUDE HORN ATHERTON,
AND THE ATHERTON HOME
AT ATHERTON, CALIFORNIA
At this home Mrs. Atherton wrote her
first novel *The Randolphs of Redwoods*.
The portrait from the author's collection;
the home photograph courtesy of
the California Historical Society.

.

MRS. GEORGE GORDON
As Elizabeth Anne Clarke, in Bow, Middlesex, England
she married George Gordon on September 17, 1843.

trude Atherton has Nina claim that her mother, out of
hatred for her father, placed whiskey in her baby food,
gradually causing Nina to become an alcoholic. This
hatred is said to have developed partially because of
George Gordon's refusal to return to England, as his
wife wished to do.

A Daughter of the Vine was published in London
and New York in 1899. In neither England nor the
United States was the new version of the Gordon story
received with much enthusiasm. The reviewer for the
English magazine *The Spectator* of March 25, 1899,
wrote: "The story inspires repulsion rather than pity.
. . . We have only to add that the reference to Branwell Bronte, who is dragged in as exercising an evil
influence on the heroine's father, seems to us most gra-
tuitous. For that we suppose we have to thank the cult
established by our native literary rag-pickers."

In America, the reviewer for *The Critic,* July 1899,
called the novel a "sad disappointment," adding that
readers had been "led to hope that her (Mrs. Atherton's) undeniable talent was at last to be rendered available for the entertainment of self-respecting readers
who do not care to penetrate the spiritual slums of life"
and that "the book is bitter and cruel, it is a perversion
of life as well as the author's talent."

Both *The Randolphs of Redwoods* and *A Daughter
of the Vine* conclude with an almost word-for-word
quotation of the San Francisco *Call* newspaper article,
"What Am I Bid?" that first inspired her to write the
Gordon story.

Mrs. Atherton often referred to the Gordon story in
her other novels. There are, for example, references in
*American Wives and English Husbands, The Califor-
nians,* and *Sisters-in-Law.* Then, late in life, at the age

of 88, she reinforced the legend in her *Golden Gate Country,* when she once more told the story of Nellie Gordon, embellishing it still further.

She had stated in her autobiography that "possibly" Gordon had known Branwell Bronte; here she declared that Gordon "was intimate with . . . Branwell." This escalation from Gordon "possibly knowing Branwell Bronte" to being "intimate" with him calls to mind Charles Dickens' description of a lantern, first referred to as "carried by my fourth son on the fifth day of November, when he was Guy Fawkes" and later as "carried by my forefather on the fifth of November and he was Guy Fawkes." Dickens refers to this change as "the exercise of a little ingenious labour on the part of the commentator."

Also, in *Golden Gate Country,* Gertrude Atherton retells the tale of the spree that led to Gordon's marriage to the barmaid and again declares that he was born in "Yorkshire, England near the village of Haworth," that he "imported the rows of ugly brown houses that encircled" South Park, that Mrs. Gordon "lived in sullen seclusion, hating everyone," and that she had "mixed whisky with (Nellie's) baby food.

Mrs. Atherton also altered her own version of Nellie's death as the years went by, the story becoming more lurid and more sensational with each retelling. In *The Randolphs of Redwood,* for instance, Nellie's uncle in a drunken rage pushes her down the stairs, fatally injuring her. Later, in her autobiography *Adventures of a Novelist,* published in 1932, she wrote that *Mrs. Gordon* "had flung Nelly down the stair." In an attempt perhaps to lend credence to this rendition, Gertrude Atherton claimed in that same book that her husband, "then little more than a boy" was present at

Nellie's deathbed. However, at the time of Nellie's death in 1874, George Atherton was actually a twenty-two year old man! Finally, in her 1945 book, *Golden Gate Country,* Nellie is reported as determined "to drink herself to death."

Of course, none of these statements is true. But more importantly, we see much that was fiction in *A Daughter of the Vine* blithely stated here as historical fact. It is in much this same manner that the legend Gertrude Atherton established has continued to grow over the years.

The tale has often been retold by others, frequently with embellishments, each one of which has added more to the legend. In the late 1940s, for instance, San Francisco *Chronicle* columnist Robert O'Brien wrote of the Gordons in his "Riptides" column and his book *This is San Francisco.* In both accounts, he followed the Atherton versions of the story, but added more fiction: Gordon sold his sugar refinery to Claus Spreckels for $500,000 and was the first to import English sparrows to California, the latter to add an English flavor to his South Park. O'Brien may have extracted the Spreckels story from a June 9, 1918, newspaper article by columnist Edward A. Morphy, but no source has been found for the allegation about the sparrows. As a matter of fact, Gordon died in 1869, and, according to Joseph Grinnell, in his authoritative *Directory of Birds of the San Francisco Region,* the first English sparrows were not seen in the Bay Area until 1871. In a more humorous vein, Ralph Hoffman wrote in his *Birds of the Pacific Coast* that they arrived "like other tramps in empty freight cars."

In 1949, Samuel Dickson titled a chapter in his *San Francisco Kaleidoscope* "Lord George Gordon." Dickson was neither the first nor the last to refer to Gordon as "Lord," but Gordon never claimed any such title, nor during his lifetime did any so refer to him. Dickson also claimed that Gordon traveled overland to California with more than $30,000 in gold; this, too, is untrue. The latter untruth probably owes its origin to a statement made in the San Francisco *Chronicle* of September 9, 1928, by E. G. Fitzhamon, who, at that time, also erroneously linked Gordon to Henry Meiggs' scheme to develop Telegraph Hill as a choice residential area and gave Gordon the undeserved honor of building Meiggs Wharf. Both of these myths were also repeated by Dickson whose version later provided the basis for a long Oakland *Tribune* article authored by The Knave and dated August 21, 1960.

In a widely circulated book about the city, *The Silent Traveler in San Francisco,* Chiang Yee repeated the usual Gordon fables, including the introduction of English sparrows. He also brought up another: "No one can tell me whether George Gordon was the first to introduce Eucalyptus trees to San Francisco," and claimed that Gordon planted Eucalyptus trees in South Park. However, there were no such trees in South Park until many years after Gordon's death, and no authority mentions Gordon introducing Eucalyptus trees to San Francisco.

Other writers, such as San Francisco's beloved Millie Robbins, Horatio F. Stoll, George Dorsey and Walter J. Thompson, also wrote about the Gordons, all following the Atherton legend, except for Stoll, whose February 24, 1907, article in the San Francisco *Sunday Call* was less lurid and more factual.

A thoroughly sensational account of the Gordons appeared in the Hearst *American Weekly* newspaper

supplement on April 10, 1950. It was one in a series
entitled "Heartbreaks of Society," written by Gene
Coughlin. The story was dramatically entitled "Elizabeth Gordon's Terrible Vow – When His Parents
Ignored Her, Gordon's Low Born Bride Decided on a
Campaign of Vengeance." Coughlin's tale begins in the
Lord Rodney Inn at Keighly when Gordon is drinking
with Branwell Bronte, and decides to marry the barmaid whom he calls Elizabeth Ann Kent. The marriage
is performed in Sheffield. Gordon's father, identified as
John Gordon, a wealthy manufacturer of nails, "was
furious when his son presented his new wife at the Gordon home in September 1844. . . he recognized her
as the barmaid of his favorite inn and refused to let her
enter the house. The other members of the household
turned their backs on the couple and the door slammed.
. . That was when Elizabeth Ann Kent Gordon took
a terrible vow, a pledge that she was not to reveal until
years later. . ." Later, in the same article, Coughlin
has Mrs. Gordon say "I have made a drunkard out of
our daughter. . . Oh, I did it craftily, I assure you,
. . . even in her gruel, in her milk, in her tea as she
grew older. I saw to it that she had a bit of rum or gin."
And so the imaginary prose continues! Coughlin concludes that South Park "is now a haven for derelicts
. . . a monument to the terrible oath."

But if Coughlin's imagination was mighty, it was no
greater than that of a more recent writer, Milla Logan.
Writing in *San Francisco Magazine* in 1965, she suggested that the "terrible curse she (Mrs. Gordon) put
on him (George Gordon) and their daughter, Nellie,
is, some say, the blight that is on South Park today."

The Gordon Legend has thus been well established
first by Gertrude Atherton's many variations on the

theme, and then embellished upon by the many subsequent writers. This writer's objective then is to present the facts he has uncovered about the Gordon family in order to separate the truth from fiction.

2

The Search for Gordon's Origin

The various lurid versions of Gordon's marriage and his wife's hatred and strange revenge seemed so sensational that they merited investigation to separate fact from fiction.

Perhaps if Gordon's early life had been less obscure, so complex a legend would not have been created. Even Gordon's birthplace had been a source of uncertainty. Was it in Scotland or England? Most Englishmen who came to California during the pioneer days and prospered left records of their origins, and their obituaries gave details of their early lives. Such is not the case with Gordon; his obituaries describe his California career but do not mention his early life. The San Francisco *Bulletin* alone ventured to name the country of his origin, noting, "He was a Scotchman by birth." This statement might have been based on the fact that Gordon was a member of the St. Andrews Society of San Francisco. Qualifications for admission were more rigid in his time than now. Members had to be Scotsmen or sons or grandsons of natives of Scotland. Now membership is open to their more distant descendants. Unfortunately, although the proceedings of the St. Andrews Society escaped destruction in the 1906 disaster, they do not give information regarding Gordon's origin. However, in an 1877 pamphlet listing all members to that date, his birthplace is given as London.

Other available records list Gordon simply as a native of Great Britain. On the headstone marking his grave at the Laurel Hill Cemetery, only his name and the dates "1820-1869" were chiseled.

In their wills, George Gordon and his wife mentioned relatives in England. Mrs. Gordon left funds for her cousin, Elizabeth Eve, of Collingham in the county of Nottinghamshire, as well as for her brother, John James Clark of Lincoln. George Gordon instructed that his three sisters, Mary S. Cummings, Adamina Cockburn and Sarah Foster (who in the end predeceased her brother) be heirs to certain shares in his sugar refinery. Only one address was given, that of Mary S. Cummings, who at the time the will was written in 1865 resided at Cecil Street, Warick Road, Carlisle, England.

Research in England was indicated. Since Gertrude Atherton had given the Haworth region of Yorkshire as the Gordons' place of origin, and Gene Coughlin, in his *American Weekly* article, had written a detailed account of events in Keighley and Sheffield and given Mrs. Gordon's maiden name as Elizabeth Ann Kent, it appeared that investigation should center in Yorkshire.

Through the kindness of the late Professor John A. Hawgood, noted specialist in Western American history at the University of Birmingham, England, the services of his students were obtained in this attempt to locate some record of Gordon's early life.

The first student, Terence M. Condon, began his research in January 1968. Birth and marriage records at the Church at Haworth (where the father of Branwell Bronte had been pastor) and nearby towns were examined, as were electoral registers, game certificates, jury lists, poor law guardians, and the records of the High Sheriff of Yorkshire, to name but a few. The files of newspapers at Sheffield were also read. No evidence was found of any Gordon who could be identified as the American immigrant of that name.

After Terence Condon left for the United States to continue his studies, his work was carried on by another student, Patrick H. Isherwood. Since Branwell Bronte had been a Mason, the records of the order in Haworth were investigated, as were the genealogical publications of the Harleian Society at the British Museum, all to no avail. Incidentally, Haworth was in the 1840s, a town which no longer was progressing, an unlikely place for the young, energetic, always ambitious Gordon to have stayed for any length of time.

In an attempt to determine the fact or fiction of Gordon's relationship with Branwell Bronte, an inquiry was sent to the eminent Bronte scholar and author of *The Brontes and Their World,* Dr. Phyllis Bentley, at her home at Halifax, Yorkshire. On January 15, 1970, Dr. Bentley replied that she could not "find any trace of him [Gordon] in works relating to the Brontes."

On January 22, she wrote further: "I have made inquiries about the George Gordons from Miss Winifred Gérin, who is the acknowledged authority in this country on the facts of the Brontes' lives. She tells me that she has never found any reference to Gordon and cannot find any reference to him in her notes. Like myself, she thinks that the story of his contact with Branwell may perhaps be a fictitious invention – after all Gertrude Atherton was a novelist!"

In 1971 the search was continued by Major W. Morice, a member of the Society of Genealogists of London. Research centered at Somerset House, where the vital statistics records of England and Wales from 1837 on are located. No records of the births or marriages of the Gordons were found.

Since Gordon's sister, Mary S. Cummings, was living in Carlisle in 1865, the city directories and marriage records were searched, as was the 1861 census, again with no results.

In his memoir of George Gordon, John T. Doyle had written that Gordon had been a "pupil of the celebrated Dr. Ure," most likely referring to Dr. Andrew Ure (1778-1857) a noted Scottish chemist, astronomer and geologist. Born in Glasgow, he had left his native city in 1830 for London. Ure had been involved in experiments with sugar, a subject familiar to Gordon. Also, Gordon had stated in testimony to a California legislative committee in 1859 that he "was educated as a civil engineer" but had not practiced that profession. Both these "leads" were explored, without results.

Major Morice was considering making further inquiries in Scotland, when he died suddenly on May 2, 1972. Mr. L. C. Suggars of Brighton then entered into the hunt for the elusive information. He proved himself to be a veritable Sherlock Holmes. After several months of fruitless search, finally in October 1972 he reported success at last! Because Gordon's sister, Mary S. Cummings, was mentioned as living in Carlisle, he did intensive work examining the records in that area. While he was searching for Mary Cummings, he discovered the death certificate of Gordon's sister, Adamina Cockburn. She had been living at Hayton, Cumberland, about six miles from Carlisle, near the Scottish border. She had died on May 12, 1874, aged forty-eight.

Further investigation resulted in finding, in the 1871 census of Hayton, some intriguing information: Adamina's husband was John Alexander Cockburn, aged fifty-six, a paper manufacturer who employed twenty-seven men, twenty-seven women, and five boys. He had been born in Carlisle; his wife Adamina's birthplace had been in London. Later it was discovered that Adamina's marriage to Cockburn had taken place on April 27, 1848, in the Presbyterian Chapel, Carlisle. At the time of his marriage Cockburn was thirty-three years old, Adamina twenty-two. Both were then residents of Carlisle. They proved childless. Cockburn died in 1884.

The Hayton census of 1871 also showed Adamina's sister, Mary S. Cummings, to be aged forty-four, a native of London, living with them. But the surprise was that Mary was listed as "unmarried." (i.e. single!) Was this a mistake? Was she a half-sister of George Gordon? Or would Gordon's name prove to be really Cummings?

Quickly the search returned to Somerset House in London. There the birth certificate of Nellie was found! She was born on August 23, 1844, at Wellington Road, in the district of Bow and Bromley, County of Middlesex – a daughter of George Gordon Cummings, a "tea and colonial broker." The long, long hunt was over – Gordon was Cummings!

The Gordons' marriage records were soon located. George Gordon Cummings had married Elizabeth Anne Clarke (spelled here with a final "e"), aged eighteen, on September 17, 1843, at the parish church at Bow, Middlesex, now part of London but then a suburb.

Gordon was a resident of Bow, while his wife was listed as residing at Haughton le Skene, county of Durham. Gordon's father was given as John Cummings, a London accountant, deceased by the date of George's marriage. George's sister, Mary S. Cummings, was a witness at her brother's marriage. Her full name was on the document; the "S" stood for Susannah.

Nellie had been baptized Helen Gordon Cummings. In California, her formal name was Helen Mae Gordon; the "Mae" must have been added later, most likely in America, as "May" was the more common spelling in England at that period.

In an effort to find more information regarding Gordon's parents, a search for a record of Gordon's own baptism was begun. There were hundreds of Established Churches in London at the time of Gordon's birth, so the quest was somewhat like looking for a needle in a haystack. Since Gordon was a member of the St. Andrews Society, as has been noted, it was possible that he, like so many other persons with origins in Scotland, had been a Presbyterian before becoming a member of the Church of England, which he was when he was married.

Mr. Suggars examined six non-conformist church registers without results. He then began the more formidable task of examining the books of the Anglican churches, starting with that in Bow, where Gordon was married and lived, then widening the search to the neighboring parishes. After he had examined the records of thirty-eight Anglican churches, the cry from England was "Eureka!" In the thirty-ninth – the Church of St. George – Gordon's baptismal record was discovered.

On April 19, 1826, four children of John and Sarah Cummings were baptized. George's birth date was given as September 27, 1818, so his age as recorded in most of the newspapers at the time of his death, on his headstone, and in other records was wrong; he was one year older. However, the removal of a year or so from one's age is not an uncommon custom.

The other Cummings children in the register were

Sarah (named after her mother), born January 8, 1820; Elizabeth Miller, born November 21, 1821; and Adamina, born January 3, 1826. Elizabeth may have died young, as there is no mention of her in George Gordon's will. Mary Susannah was not born until 1827, and she was not baptized at St. George's. Gordon was baptized George Cummings, so the "Gordon" given as his middle name in his marriage record must have been added between the two events.

Gordon's parents, John and Sarah Cummings, were living on Cleveland Street, Mile End, at the time of the baptisms. Mile End was a rural area at this time. The parish church of Mile End was St. Dunstons, Spepney, and in its register are recorded the deaths of Sarah Cummings, originally of Ratcliff, who died on November 23, 1831, aged 33, and John Cummings, who died on October 25, 1829, aged 38.

When George Gordon was admitted to the freedom of the City of London in January 1844, he declared his father was "late of Edinboro, a brewer, deceased." A careful search of the records in Edinburgh, Scotland, failed to disclose any information about John Cummings. The quest returned to the Carlisle region and there again the research was fruitful. The book of marriage bans of Carlisle recorded that on January 1, 1818, John Cummings, a "common Brewer, of the Swan Brewery, High Street, Whitechapel, London," married Sarah, daughter of Joseph Waugh of St. Cuthbert's Parish, who was a grocer. The name of Waugh, fairly common in the north of England, is of Scottish origin.

The London directories of 1818 and 1819 list John Cummings with the Swan "Brewhouse." However, a change in his occupation is noted in the 1827 directory. There he is listed as "accountant" of 15 London Street,

in business on his own. This address is near Mincing
Lane and St. Botolph's Lane, not far from St. George's
Church where his children were baptized. These records relating to Gordon's parents give further indication of his solid middle-class background.

As to Mrs. George Gordon, in her will, already mentioned, her brother John James Clark was noted as living in Lincoln. The 1861 Lincoln census was examined,
and Clark was found to be at 236 High Street, in the
parish of St. Peter-at-Arches. He was unmarried, a
clerk, born at Market Rasen, Lincolnshire, about twenty
miles from Lincoln.

Through the kindness of the vicar of Market Rasen,
Reverend F. E. Stalley, more material was found on
George Gordon's wife herself. Elizabeth Anne Clark
had been born May 26, 1825, and her brother John
James Clark on June 26, 1828. Another brother, Rich-
ard, born November 9, 1827, had presumably died
young. Their parents were John James Clark and Mary
Clark.

The senior John James Clark was a draper and
mercer at Market Rasen. At the age of 28 years, on
June 24, 1818, he had married Mary Mawer, aged 21.
Her father was also a draper and mercer who in 1810
had established his own business. In 1822 he invested in
it 12,800 pounds, a not inconsiderable sum at that time,
and took as a partner Joseph Collingham, his one-time
apprentice and later son-in-law. The firm of Mawer
and Collingham, now a large department store, is still
in existence in Lincoln and still owned by the same
family.

By the time of George Gordon's marriage to Elizabeth Anne Clark in 1843, her father was listed as
"gentleman," that is, a man of property, of independent
means.

In the Collingham census of 1871, information regarding Elizabeth Anne Clark's cousin, Elizabeth Eve, was found. At that date she was 47 years old, married to John Eve, a "silk Mercer" and they had four children and two servants. She, too, had been born at Market Rasen. Her father was John Cumpstone, a surgeon. He had married Mrs. Gordon's aunt, Elizabeth Clark, on May 31, 1821. Both John Cumpstone and later his son William practiced medicine at Market Rasen.

Thus it is readily evident that the family of Mrs. Gordon was equal and most probably superior in its social standing to that of Gordon. The status of her various relatives renders further proof of the ridiculousness of the bar maid myth.

The search then returned to Gordon. A new attempt was made to determine if Gordon, under his correct name of Cummings, had associated with the Brontes. Again there was no evidence found. Dr. Phyllis Bentley wrote: "I cannot find any trace of George Gordon Cummings either in the official Bronte biographies or in my own Bronte notes." Branwell was in London in 1835 where he frequented the Castle Tavern in Holborn. However, in 1835 Gordon was only sixteen years old. In 1843, Branwell was a tutor at Thorp Green, twelve miles from York. Gordon was married September 17 of that year. Bronte does not appear to have been in Haworth or Keighley in September.

Thus the legend of Gordon's marriage to a barmaid after a drunken spree (with Branwell Bronte) appears thoroughly unfounded. It fails in a number of aspects. They are:

(1) In England, after 1756, one could not get married on the spur of the moment. If one was married by

license, the waiting period was at least two days after application to the representative of the area Bishop. Gordon was married in an Anglican Church, "according to the rites and ceremonies of the Established Church of England," and normally Anglican marriage was by "bans" which were called three times in the church, there being a week between each calling. A civil marriage at a registrar's office required one full day's notice.

(2) One cannot imagine John Clark, businessman and "gentleman," permitting his daughter to be a barmaid.

(3) As Elizabeth Anne was a minor, consent to her marriage had to be given by her father.

(4) Neither Gordon nor his bride was a resident of Yorkshire in 1843. Even if they had been in Haworth or Keighley and Gordon had gone on a spree, it is unlikely they would have traveled the long distance of more than 200 miles by horse-drawn coach to be married in London.

Since it appears the Gordons had no association with the Brontes, why did Gertrude Atherton introduce Branwell Bronte into the story? Was it that, as Kevin Starr wrote in discussing her writings, "excluded from history, Atherton returned to myth." She had been fascinated with the Bronte sisters since the age of fourteen when she first read *Jane Eyre*. In fact she related in her autobiography that she read the novel six times. In her voluminous writings she often referred to the Bronte sisters, and sometimes to the black sheep Branwell.

In her novel about the Gordons, *The Randolphs of Redwoods,* Gertrude Atherton describes a scene of the drunken beast-like Mrs. Gordon being seen by the hero, Colonel St. John – a scene quite similar to Jane Eyre viewing the mad wife of her beloved Rochester. Even the name of Colonel St. John, the hero in Gertrude's story, is a name of an important character in Charlotte Bronte's *Jane Eyre*.

Did she, as a young woman, dream of emulating the Brontes and becoming a woman author? Gertrude Atherton became a liberated woman; the Brontes did not, but each of the Brontes was considered, as was Mrs. Atherton, "an unwomanly woman writer."

Another perplexing question is why Gordon changed his name. John T. Doyle in his sketch of Gordon wrote that he "had been in, I know not what, business in England. I conjecture that his place was seized by the Government for some violation of the Revenue law, and either for that or some other reason he came to the U.S."

As Gordon was a "Tea and Colonial Broker," a middle-man between the importer of tea and the shop-keeper or wholesaler, he might have tried to smuggle tea. This was not an unusual thing; it has been said, "the English have always eyed smuggling-in as a worthy pastime." However, the Petty Sessions Records at the Mansion House Court (Mincing Lane, Gordon's address, is within its jurisdiction) show no misdemeanor by George Gordon Cummings between November 1845 and November 1847, the years before the probable date of his emigration to the United States.

It is unlikely that Gordon committed any major crime, as he returned to England in 1865, and possibly also in 1860. He remained in England most of the time from 1865 to 1867, and contracted various business transactions without difficulty.

The changing of names by California pioneers was

not an unusual occurrence. A few notable examples were Henry Miller, the "cattle king," born Heinrich Alfred Kreiser. The change to Henry Miller was merely for convenience in obtaining a ticket to California. Talbot Green (for whom San Francisco's Green Street is named) has a far different story; while a candidate for mayor, he was recognized as Paul Geddes, a Philadelphia embezzler! The original name of Thomas H. Blythe, for whom the California city of Blythe is named, was found to be Williams. Andrew Hallidie, the inventor of the San Francisco cable cars was baptized Andrew Hallidie Smith.

It was no wonder a popular ballad of Gold Rush days went:

> Oh, what was your name in the States?
> Was it Muggins or Buggins or Bates?
> Did you murder your wife and fly for your life?
> Say, what was your name in the States?

On his 1843 marriage certificate Gordon is called a "colonial broker." On his daughter's baptismal certificate of August 1844, he is listed as "tea and colonial broker;" and the Post Office London Directory of 1845 lists him as a "tea and col. and guano brokr" doing business at 14 Mincing Lane. In the same directory in the town of Bow, where he lived, there are 73 names under the classification "Gentry" and about 150 "Traders." The "traders" were green-grocers, cheese mongers, surgeons, linen drapers, and the like. No occupation is given for those listed as "gentry," which includes "G. Gordon Cummings, esq. Wellington rd."

Gordon's 1844 admission to "the freedom of the City" carried certain privileges including the right to exercise a trade and to vote at local elections, immunity from tolls at all markets and fairs in England, and freedom from impressment into the armed forces. In that same year, he was licensed as a broker, although he had apparently been operating in that occupation earlier. Nevertheless, in his petition dated January 30, which is in the Corporation of London Record Office, his occupation is given as "spectaclemaker." Since Gordon has referred to himself as a "Colonial Broker," six months before his license was issued, one wonders if his father-in-law provided the cash needed for his advancement from spectaclemaker to broker. His petition having been allowed at the end of February, a bond of 1,000 pounds was placed on March 9 to assure his license.

It is significant that while in America Gordon called himself an engineer, real estate broker, chemist, geologist, contractor, etc., he never referred in any manner to his occupations of tea or guano broker or spectaclemaker. He may not have been in this latter pursuit any length of time, as his name is not listed in the records of the Guild of Spectaclemakers.

The 1846 London Directory, probably compiled in late 1845, lists George Gordon Cummings as a broker, still at the same address, 14 Mincing Lane, but he is not listed in the 1847 or 1848 directories. In 1847, 14 Mincing Lane was occupied by, among others, Hulbert Layton and Company, Tea and Colonial Brokers. Gordon may have sold his business to that firm. It is of interest that Mincing Lane is still the headquarters of the English tea trade.

Many years later Gordon testified in a law case that he had resided in India a short time. However, in the Records of India filed at the Society of Genealogists in England, George Gordon Cummings is not listed, nor has his name been found in the records of the India

Office Library, London, among those arriving in India in the period 1836-1842.

In John T. Doyle's manuscript life of Gordon, it is claimed he arrived in New York in 1847, and on arrival, read in the New York *Tribune* a letter from Professor Mapes concerning agricultural chemistry, to which Gordon responded in a letter to the newspaper, enlarging on Mapes' discussion. The editor, Horace Greeley (wrote Doyle) being impressed, arranged for an interview with Gordon, which resulted in Gordon writing weekly letters to the *Tribune*. Because of the possibility that he might have arrived in 1846, a careful search of that year's *Tribune* for Cummings and Gordon was undertaken. Neither it nor the 1847 issues substantiated Doyle's assertion. When Greeley visited San Francisco in 1859, Gordon was not a member of the committee to welcome him. Greeley's book *An Overland Journey from New York to San Francisco in the Summer of 1859* mentions some of the industries of San Francisco, but there is no account of Gordon's sugar refinery. Gordon was an inveterate letter writer to the newspapers, so he may have written to New York newspapers, possibly some other paper than the *Tribune*. Doyle was quite elderly when he wrote his account of Gordon, and Gordon had been dead over thirty years.

Testifying in a court case, Gordon stated he had "resided in New York and Philadelphia and my business was that of a dealer in real estate and a civil engineer."

Only one George Gordon (and no George Cummings) who might be "our" Gordon appears in the New York City directories. This George Gordon, listed in 1848 and 1849, but not in 1850, was an "agent" with offices at 78 Brook Street and a residence on Staten

Island. There is no information at the New York Historical Society nor at the New York Public Library regarding George Gordon or his California Association, an emigrating company he formed in 1848.

A member of Gordon's California Association, Atkins Massey, a Philadelphian, claimed in an interview a number of years after Gordon's death that Gordon, after he "arrived in Philadelphia from England," had been involved in Pennsylvania coal properties, losing considerable money. This statement has often been repeated. The amount of money lost by Gordon could not have been great if Doyle's account is true, as Doyle wrote that Gordon arrived in America without funds.

Neither is Gordon (nor Cummings) listed in the Philadelphia city directories, or in the catalogue of the Free Library of Philadelphia or the Historical Society of Pennsylvania at Philadelphia.

The Pennsylvania Archives and the catalogue of the State Library, located at Harrisburg, were also examined, but no reference to Gordon or Cummings was found.

The exact date of the arrival of the Gordons in the United States, and when Cummings changed his name to Gordon have not been learned. His life on the eastern seaboard is not documented until the California Gold Rush. However, judging from Gordon's California career it is quite certain that his life must have been one of intensive activity.

3

Ho! for California

In 1848 the epic drama of the world's greatest gold rush was about to unfold. Slowly, the fantastic tale of the discovery in January at Sutter's mill began to spread throughout the nation, causing ever increasing excitement.

Finally, on December 5, President Polk, in his message to Congress, confirmed the rumors in provocative words: "The accounts of the abundance of gold in that territory are of such an extraordinary character as would scarcely command belief were they not corroborated by the authentic reports of officers in the public service, who have visited the mineral district, and derived the facts which they detail from personal observation." The result was, as Victor Berthold wrote in his history of the first Panama-to-San Francisco steamship, an "emotional tidal wave that swept over the world." The Gold Rush was on; the cry was "Ho! for California!"

George Gordon, young and vigorous, had little to hold him to the eastern shore. Here was an opportunity to gain riches, and he was not one to hesitate to seize it. Gordon in 1855 wrote, "I came [to California] from reading sundry pamphlets containing Governor Mason's report, T. O. Larkin's letters and President Polk's message."

On December 14, only nine days after President Polk's message, a notice appeared in the Philadelphia *Public Ledger* announcing the formation of "Gordon's California Association."

Ferol Egan, in *The El Dorado Trail,* described leaders similar in type to Gordon as "sellers of the Dream." Egan wrote of men of "commanding presence and ability to assume leadership" who became "salesmen for the new El Dorado" and who implied to prospective emigrants that the trip there "would be easy — oh, so easy."

Associations like Gordon's, formally organized with quotas of members, officers and agreed upon rules, were common during the gold rush. The New York *Herald* of January 24, 1849, listed forty-seven companies, including Gordon's, all bound for the gold fields. Each was formed with the intention of working as a unit, not only on the journey to California but in the mining regions as well. They took with them strange and wonderful machinery for extracting gold, and enough provisions not only to last the entire trip but often, as Gordon claimed he would, enough for "three months after arrival at San Francisco." Gordon also claimed in his announcement that "a company under adequate guidance will be more profitable and much safer than random personal exertion."

Actually the gold-seekers' companies, regardless of their agreements, broke up before or upon arrival in California. To quote a leading historian of the gold rush, Rodman Paul, "The elaborate charters and constitutions under which most of them were supposed to operate had been drawn up by persons ignorant of California conditions." The mining machinery, found worthless, was left to rust on the beaches of San Francisco, while the provisions were usually exhausted long before the voyages ended. Gordon's expedition was no exception.

In his numerous newspaper notices in Philadelphia

TO CALIFORNIA
ON SHARES.

TO SAIL ON JANUARY 15th.

Entire Expense for Passage and Outfit $160.

A few persons of industrious habits and who can give undoubted references of their good moral character, can join

GORDON'S
CALIFORNIA ASSOCIATION.

This Association consists of **100** members who go in a body well armed, whose object is to go safely, and comfortably fitted out and equipped.

Each member pays **$160**, for which he has passage in a fast sailing vessel, and is found with six months' provisions of the best quality.

The President of the Company, who is a practical geologist, accompanies the expedition, and for the one-fifth share in the profit provides the Association with

CAMP EQUIPMENT,

To every ten men a large tent with oil skin cover.

To every man a hammock, hammock bed, blankets and coverlid, a tin plate, dish, mug, knives and forks, &c.

To every twenty men a Field Cooking Stove, ovens, boilers and kettles. Also,

MACHINERY AND IMPLEMENTS:

Machines for washing in the gold deposits to go by horse power, force pumps, screens, seives, shovels, pick axes, axes, saws, two sets carpenters tools, set of coopers tools, set of blacksmiths tools, including forge, bellows, &c. saddlers and sailmakers tools, tinsmiths tools, &c. saddles and bridles, rifles, fowling pieces, fishing tackle, and agricultural implements.

The Association carries a complete medicine chest and a Physician.

A German assayer with chemical tests and apparatus for trying the value of minerals.

The main body of the Association go by Cape Horn, and a few go across by Mexico as pioneers, to survey locations and prepare the way for the arrival of the rest of the company.

The great object of the Association is, by combining together to make a strong party to insure the *safety* of every member, to have all the assistance that good machinery and science can give in washing for gold, and to have everything comfortable and convenient, so that the trip may be made reasonably pleasant. Good care will be taken of health, and all be brought within a small expense.

The agent of the Association is now in California and doing well.

Apply immediately and if possible personally, at the office of the Association.

A. COCHRANE'S,

143 Walnut St. 2 doors above Sixth, Phila.

The Articles of Association can be seen by calling upon

GORDON'S 1849 BROADSIDE OF HIS CALIFORNIA ASSOCIATION
From the author's collection.

and New York, Gordon termed himself a "geologist" and "inventor of an approved machine for separating gold dust." He claimed his association would have "perfect camp equipment and horse power machinery;" that his agent "is in California and has been succesful in the gold deposits." He referred to his "shipping line," stating that an "agent of the line has gone to charter a vessel on the Pacific side." These flamboyant announcements were, however, without substance.

Gordon's early newspaper notices referred to his association as a Philadelphia organization; one in the New York *Herald* did so as late as December 28, 1848. The Philadelphia agents were given as Wm. Goodrich and Co. of 116 Market Street and Andrew Cochrane of 143 Walnut Street.

By the beginning of 1849, however, Gordon's Association had become a New York *and* Philadelphia company, with a New York agent, W. C. Ulhorn, of 106 Front Street.

Although on the frontier and in middle America the overland route to California was popular, in the states along the Atlantic, the ocean was the favored route. This was the route Gordon chose.

In addition to the notices which appeared in the newspapers during the next couple of months puffing his California Association, Gordon himself also distributed broadsides telling of the plans and benefits of his company. One of the broadsides was obtained by the author at the famous Thomas Streeter auction of Western Americana in 1968. It is reproduced in this volume as one of the illustrations.

John T. Doyle, in his sketch of Gordon, related an incident regarding the formation of the association. He stated that Gordon called a meeting in New York of

those interested in going to California. To a full room
he explained his scheme and the expenses. Doyle wrote:
"Then began questions such as the American people
only know how to ask. He stood on that little platform
for an hour and a half undergoing cross-examination at
the hands of everyone in the audience who was of an
investigating turn of mind. He answered as well as he
could and of course turned out to know more about the
matter than anyone in the crowd."

Gordon decided his party would sail from New
York, and on January 10, 1849, his advertisement in the
New York *Herald* declared confidently: "Splendid
white-oak built ship *Clarissa Perkins* lying in New
York, is chartered to convey this Association . . .
She is commanded by Capt. James W. Goodrich, one
of the members, an experienced Cape Horn and Pacific
Captain, who has some of the shortest passages on
record." On the 16th Gordon added: "Lots will be
drawn for choice of berths when all are aboard." The
original sailing date was announced as January 16.
However, fourteen days later, on January 30, a notice
appeared that "This Association has its full comple-
ment of 150 members" and would sail via Cape Horn
on February 2. All members were invited to a "Farewell Supper on the evening of 1st Feb., on Board the
Clarissa Perkins in New York."

Finally on February 8 the *Clarissa Perkins* sailed for
California. Built in Maine nine years earlier and dis-
placing 240 tons, she carried 127 passengers.

> Oh California,
> That's the Land for me;
> I'm off for California
> With my wash bowl on my knee!

The *Clarissa Perkins* was to go around Cape Horn

and up the West Coast to San Francisco. Several weeks before she sailed, Gordon had called for the election of an additional "committee" of association members to disembark in Mexico and proceed to California overland. That plan was not carried out, but five days before the *Clarissa Perkins* cleared the New York harbor on February 3, in the Philadelphia *Public Ledger* he explained details of a new plan:

> Arrangements have been made to form a second company of one hundred strong on the same basis as Gordon's California Association, which has been so universally approved. To go overland, the safest and best route by Lake Nicaragua in sixty-five days to San Francisco, President Gordon will make all the arrangements necessary for said company on the Pacific and Lakes by a speedy and safe conveyance to California.

This was the company that was to sail, with Gordon himself, on the brig *Mary*. His plan was that he and the members of this second company would arrive in San Francisco in time to await the *Clarissa Perkins* carrying the supplies and mining machinery. When she arrived, all would then be in readiness for the departure for the gold fields.

A New York *Herald* advertisement headed *"Ho for California"* gave the rates of the second contingent. "Passage with board on the road, and three months provisions after arrival at San Francisco, $225, with state rooms, $260." This was considerably more expensive than the $160 required for the *Clarissa Perkins* passage. In subsequent notices, Gordon explained that the route across Nicaragua "is 1,000 miles nearer than by Chagres [Panama] and with less land transit" and that this was the "healthy route." The Panama crossing was, in fact, through a cholera-ridden country, while Nicaragua was free of this scourge until 1852.

The *Mary* was scheduled to sail on February 5, but on February 10 the New York *Herald* carried a notice that "the President of Gordon's California Association goes out in the Brig *Mary* and has soundings and surveys of the entire route. Apply on board the *Mary,* pier 15, foot of Wall Street." Finally, on February 21 she cleared the harbor. The *Herald* carried a list of her 116 passengers and the name of her Captain, J. K. Hayes. Among the *Mary's* passengers were not only George Gordon himself, but his wife and four-year-old daughter as well.

The official record of the voyage of the *Clarissa Perkins* with the first division no longer exists. The log, written by Samuel H. Jarden (or Jorden) of Philadelphia was presented to the Society of California Pioneers during the centennial year of 1876. After George Gordon's death, Mrs. Gordon gave the Pioneers the complete records of the trip, including the contract and by-laws. All were destroyed in the 1906 San Francisco disaster.

The long voyage around the Horn to California was always marked by tedious days of utter boredom. Passengers complained of the poor quality of the food, and the often meager allotment of water. There was also danger, especially rounding the Cape; it was usually a storm-lashed passage. Members of Gordon's group made the same complaints as almost all the other seaborne gold seekers.

One of the accounts of the voyage of the *Clarissa Perkins* appeared in the San Jose *Pioneer,* February 22, 1879, following the thirtieth anniversary of the ship's departure from New York. The occasion had been commemorated with a dinner at the Maison Dorée in San Francisco. The article related that most of the *Clarissa*

Perkins' passengers were from Pennsylvania, but, because of fear of ice in the Delaware, they went to New York to sail. It claimed the passengers numbered 132. (The New York newspapers of 1849 gave the total as 127, while the San Francisco papers stated 119 arrived on September 12, 1849.) One death occurred, that of George C. Little, a confectioner of Baltimore. On June 29, while trying to catch "Cape pigeons," he fell overboard and drowned. Because of the high seas, an approaching storm, and the poor condition of the life boats, no rescue was possible.

An article in the San Francisco *Call* of November 28, 1886, gave some additional information regarding the voyage. The reporter wrote that he had "stumbled on a pretentious looking document in old English letters formed by pen. . . yellow with age." It was a "prolix contract" dated January 11, 1849, giving the terms of Gordon's agreement with the association's members. According to these terms, Gordon would provide passage, and on arrival in California, tents and tools. Every company of ten men would receive two of Gordon's gold washing machines. In return, Gordon was to receive one fifth of all gold obtained. This arrangement was not unusual. Roger Baldwin, a member of the second contingent of Gordon's association, wrote in 1849 of a Captain Montague who was taking forty passengers to California on his ship; he was to receive "one half of the profits in the gold fields for two years."

The *Call* reporter interviewed Atkins Massey, who had been a passenger on the *Clarissa Perkins* and in San Francisco had become a well known undertaker. (Mark Twain once ridiculed him as a "corpse planter.") Massey claimed Gordon was "in cahoots with Goodrich, the captain" and that the *Clarissa*

Perkins was "a dirty old tub, not fit to accommodate fifty passengers." He reported that, "a few of the members backed square out and forfeited their advance to Gordon" and that there "were only six men in the crew, there was no one to cook for us and the ship was filthy enough to breed a pestilence." Massey's statement is at variance with the New York newspaper of February 1849, which gave the number of the crew members as seventeen. Massey also stated that off the coast of Brazil near Cape St. Rogue "the Captain missed his reckoning on his course, and we remained becalmed thirty days . . . and the sun hot enough, if we left the shade, to fry one's brains into an omelette." When asked about the Gordon contract, Massey replied it did not amount to "a handful of sand from one of the Cliff House dunes." He concluded that the passengers of the *Clarissa Perkins* were for stringing Captain Goodrich to the yardarm. He also claimed the members of the second section, aboard the *Mary,* "were selecting lariats strong enough to hang Gordon." Massey was most critical of the slowness of the *Clarissa Perkins* voyage.

Yet, according to 1849 accounts in the San Francisco newspapers, the *Clarissa Perkins'* time was not very much longer than most – 216 days from New York. Other ships arriving from New York on the same day, September 12, took 206 days and 200 days, while one from Boston took 212 days. John E. Pomfret in his *California Gold Rush Voyages* stated the average time was 199 days, while Ernest A. Wiltsee wrote in *Gold Rush Steamers* that it was 150 to 200 days.

At Rio de Janeiro the *Clarissa Perkins* had encountered the California-bound ships *Morrison* and *Mason.* The *Morrison* arrived in San Francisco eight days after the *Clarissa Perkins,* the *Mason* a month later, on October 12.

William F. Swasey, in his book *Early Days and Men of California,* published in 1891, shed further light on Massey's own trip to California. Swasey wrote that Massey and twelve other passengers of the *Clarissa Perkins* were "basely deserted in a foreign port [Rio de Janeiro] without any means" while "the captain in a drunken fit, cooly put to sea." However, they were able to secure passage on the *Samoset* which arrived in San Francisco Bay three days before the *Clarissa Perkins,* September 9.

In 1888, G. W. Sullivan had written in a similar vein of this episode of Massey's desertion in Rio. These, and all the other printed California accounts of the voyage of the *Clarissa Perkins,* have echoed Massey's derogatory view, which was perhaps caused by chagrin at being left behind. Massey was on the ship for a comparatively short time, and his statements were made years later. In contrast were the contemporary descriptions which appeared in the New Haven newspapers in 1849, written by members who made the entire trip.

There was a sizable number of Connecticut men on the *Clarissa Perkins.* Possibly some were drawn to the voyage by an article which appeared in the New Haven *Columbian Register* on January 27, 1849, stating the *Clarissa Perkins* was "commanded by one of our own townsmen, Captain Goodrich, who is well known as a thorough sailor, a competent officer and a courteous and agreeable gentleman."

On June 23, 1849, in this same newspaper, there appeared a letter from Rio de Janeiro dated May 30, written by a New Haven lad, O. S. Gilbert. A member of Gordon's association, he related his experiences on board ship during the first half of the voyage:

"It was found necessary in a company of 120 persons

to have some laws by which to be governed. . . Hence a legislature was established consisting of thirteen members." Massey's name is not on the list, although in 1886 he stated that he had been elected the "ship's majordomo" and had straightened out problems.

Gilbert wrote that a newspaper was brought "into existence under the editorship of the captain" which served "to while away many hours which would otherwise have hung heavy upon our hands." In Rio, according to his account, there were several California vessels carrying passengers returning to the States, but the passengers of the *Clarissa Perkins* were continuing onward, "resolved not to look back."

Another passenger on the *Clarissa Perkins,* George Jerome of New Haven, kept an account of the voyage which he sent to the *Daily Palladium* of New Haven on arrival in San Francisco. This letter of over 1,300 words was published on December 12, 1849. His account of the association's departure from Rio differs from Massey's report that he was "basely deserted." Jerome wrote, "we left Rio very suddenly in consequence of one of our company, Sam Badger, Jr., drawing a pistol upon the emperor's guard; and if we had not escaped as we did, we should not have got away at all, yet I am sorry to say we left seven of our best men behind, in making our escape."

He criticized the food and water vividly: "The stewards had but little trouble going after their meat, for it would sometimes meet them, after walking as fast as their pursuers; and as for the water, it was black as ink and of such disgusting smell, that the only way we could drink it was through the spout of a tea-kettle."

As the vessel neared California, food became "so scarce we have become almost anihilated. It really does seem as if we had nothing for breakfast, boil it for dinner, hash it for supper. . . If the musty tack does not keep us alive, the excitement will, so hurrah for the Golden Land."

On September 9, he wrote, "We have had head winds and were blown near the Sandwich Islands gaining only 17 miles in two weeks." But then, three days later, it was, "We are here – the goal is won – the victory ours." They had arrived on the "glittering soil of California."

Although the discomforts of the long passage were many, Jerome had praise for the officers and crew, stating that it was "through the instrumentality of the best officers and the most daring and intrepid seamen that ever sailed the ocean" that they made the voyage safely. His general conclusion was that the *Clarissa Perkins,* "under the command of our skillful captain . . . proved herself a good sea vessel."

Of the trip to California of the second section of the Gordon Association fuller details have come down to us. On February 10, 1849, eleven days before the brig *Mary* sailed, the New York *Tribune* carried an article which reads, in part: "About a dozen of Reading's townsmen form part of a company of 150, organized in Philadelphia and New York under title of the 'Gordon California Association' the President of which is George Gordon, Esq., a practical Geologist and a good business man. . . They go from New York to the mouth of the San Juan River, thence by Steamboats which they take with them, up that river to Lake Nicaragua, striking the town of Grenada [*sic*] whence they will take a well traveled carriage road of 60 miles, through Central America, to Realejo, a town on the Pacific of some 32,000 inhabitants. . . By this route they expect to avoid all the difficulties and dangers of the Chagres route, and calculate to reach their destination in 50 or 60 days at the farthest." They of course did not.

The *Mary* sailed from New York on February 21, 1849, with 116 passengers. Ray A. Billington in his classic *The Far Western Frontier* wrote of departures such as the *Mary's:* "The docks at New York and Philadelphia and Boston were jammed with starry-eyed men and teary-eyed women, as ship after ship sailed away."

Fortunately, a vivid description of the sailing of the *Mary* itself and the Gordon family has come down to us in a letter written by Henrietta Blake, the sister of Charles T. Blake, who was a passenger. She wrote it only five days after the sailing, to another brother, George. She told of the delays in the sailing of the *Mary,* and that she found it "a much smaller ship than I had supposed." The stateroom for her brother and his two Yale classmates, Roger Baldwin and Edwin (Ned) Tyler, is described as "rather small" with three berths, but "just right" and "one of the best, it being the largest and in the center of the ship." She wrote of the dissatisfaction of the passengers at being delayed in New York – "an expense, and they felt as if they could ill afford it. . . They "vowed vengeance on Mr. Gordon. . ." Finally the Gordons themselves arrived with their fellow passengers, the Stillmans, and Miss Blake's description is most intriguing when one recalls the Gertrude Atherton legend:

> And in came Mrs. Gordon and Mrs. Stillman and Mr. Stillman carrying Mrs. Gordon's little girl, a sweet little thing about four years old. We were very much pleased with Mrs. Gordon and Mrs. Stillman; they are very ladylike and agreeable. . . Mrs. Gordon is a young English lady about twenty-five, I should think, exceedingly graceful and refined in her appearance. . .

Then Mr. Gordon came on board and we were perfectly charmed with him. I was entirely captivated and carried away – he is the handsomest man I ever saw and he managed that impatient crowd so admirably that I saw he was just the one to take charge of such an enterprise – he is quite young though. . .

[She described the sailing of the *Mary*] Then such cheering and hurrahing for everything and everybody – every face was radiant with happiness and expectation. . . Then came the parting – it was sad but still full of hope we said good bye to them and the ropes were drawn in and we receded from them. . . We watched the ship as long as it was visible and saw it at last drop down behind the line of the horizon – and so he had gone. . . God will take care of him and bring him back to us, I know.

Several members of that second section of the company left accounts of it. The best known is *Tarrying in Nicaragua* which appeared in *The Century Magazine* in October 1891. This was written by the same Roger Sherman Baldwin Jr. mentioned by Miss Blake. Baldwin's family was most prominent in Connecticut, where his father had served as governor, and in 1849 was a United States Senator. The reasons Baldwin gave in the article for young men going to California are meaningful, echoing as they do the desires of youth. He wrote, "They did not go primarily to dig for gold. With some of them that was but a remote contingency. But their professional studies were completed, their old companionship was broken up, and they were feeling the sense of isolation and discouragement inevitable to the early months of professional life, when all business worth having seems already captured by the older and more experienced."

From the Baldwin family papers at Yale University Library, one learns of Roger's search for a suitable company with which to journey to California. At first, he considered the Panama route, but on hearing of the "thousands" waiting in Panama for a ship to San Francisco, considered others, including "through Nicaragua Lake to Realejo," and the route from Vera Cruz across Mexico. In a letter of January 21, he mentioned receiving from his father a circular "of Captain Goodrich's on the Gordon Association," describing the plans for the two sections.

So finally Baldwin and his Yale classmates decided to join the Gordon company because of "the interesting character of the region to be crossed, together with the pleasing address and beguiling promises of the projectors of the enterprise."

On February 3 young Baldwin wrote his father that he and Charles Blake had engaged berths on Gordon's brig *Mary*. He gave the presence of cholera in the Isthmus as one of the deciding factors. Apparently speed was another. "Mr. Gordon feels confident," he wrote, "that the trip to San Francisco will be made in less than sixty days." He added, "We anticipate quite a pleasant little trip."

The receipt given Baldwin when he paid for his passage carried the actual terms Gordon offered and required of members of the second section.

State Room Passage.
GORDON'S PASSENGER LINE
to
SAN FRANCISCO, VIA LAKE NICARAGUA AND REALEJO.

Received of Roger S. Baldwin, Jr., *the sum of one hundred and thirty dollars being in part for his passage* to San Francisco, *in the above line.*

On payment of Balance, One Hundred and Thirty Dollars, This Receipt secures to him passage in the *Mary,* Captain Hayes, from New York to San Juan de Nicaragua, from thence per Steam Boat *Plutus* to GRANADA, on Lake Nicaragua; or, navigation permitting, to Managua, Matiares or Nagarote on

Lake Leon, as may be most convenient for landing; and a passage from Realejo, on the Pacific, to San Francisco, with Hammock, Bed, and Bedding for the voyage, and Camp accommodations during detention on land, *en route*.

The following provisions will be provided, viz:

For Breakfast. – *Coffee and White Sugar – Ham, Fish, Sausages – White Biscuit – half a pound Preserved Fruit to each ten persons.*

For Dinner. – *One third of a quart of Soup made from* Kensett & Co.'s preserved Soups – *Salt Beef or Pork – Potatoes, Hominy, Peas, or Rice – Rice or Flour Puddings.*

For Supper. – *Tea and White Sugar – Ham, Fish, or Sausage – White Biscuit – half a pound of Fruit Marmalade to each ten persons.*

The above is to be served up during the voyages, and on the Lake and Land transit, circumstances permitting.

Saloon Passengers will be expected to form into Messes, and the Gentlemen in rotation to receive and serve up their own meals from the Cooks (in the manner pursued in the U.S. Service). Passengers who take State Rooms will have a Steward provided who will expect a fee of $5 from each passenger. The provisions are alike in both cases.

One Hundred Pounds of personal Baggage will be carried free if packed in round covered Valises or Bags weighing not more than 125 lb. each package; freight above that weight taken at $6 per 100 lb. Passengers are expected to assist in packing, stowing and unloading Baggage and provisions if necessary.

Any extra charges for passports, or transit Duties to be borne by each passenger. The general Customs Business will be transacted by an agent of the Line at San Juan or San Carlos without charge.

Gentlemen Passengers, if required, will have to walk from Granada or Lake Leon to Realejo 1½ or 3 days' march).

The Line provides an agent to charter vessels at Panama, Acapulco, and other Pacific Ports, so as to avoid detention at Realejo.

In the *unexpected* event of Vessels not being procured, $75 of the passage money and 60 days' provisions will be refunded to each passenger at Realejo, which will procure passage in the Mail Steamers which touch there.

On the arrival of the passengers at San Francisco each passenger will have handed to him

1 Barrel White Biscuit.

½ Barrel Flour.

1 ½ lb. of Tea, in ½ lb. leaden packages.

6 lb. of Ground Coffee, in 1 lb. leaden packages.

15 lb. White Sugar.

1 Cheese (boxed up) about twenty pounds.

Which will furnish one person with all necessary provisions, except meat, for three months.

Every Gentleman passenger is required to provide himself with a Rifle or Musket. All Powder must positively be placed in the hands of the Agent of the line.

GEO. GORDON.

On February 12, nine days before sailing, Baldwin wrote his mother saying he had heard that obtaining passage from Realejo was not as easy as first expected, "but it is too late now." On February 15, he wrote his father more hopefully: "It is certainly for Mr. Gordon's interest to get us to San Francisco as soon as possible, for if our detention is long, the support of seventy or eighty men will be no small burden on him, and I had understood that he had taken measures which should almost insure the presence of a vessel at Realejo after our arrival."

The first of Baldwin's letters at Yale University Library which describes the trip was written March 20 from San Juan de Nicaragua (del Norte), the city also known as Greytown. He stated the group had arrived there after a fairly uneventful trip, and he described San Juan as a pleasant place. His letter of May 24, from Granada, however, reflects his disgust with the progress: ". . . it is too true that although 'sixty days' and thirty more have elapsed, I am no further advanced than this old city." He explained that their steamboat, the *Plutus,* proved worthless, and many proceeded up the San Juan River in bungos, crude dugout canoes, then sailed across lake Nicaragua to Granada.

Although the statement did not appear in his *Century Magazine* article, Baldwin's letters carried a critical comment on Gordon: "The truth is that we have been under the guidance of a man who combines a little of the knave and a great deal of the fool, who in trying to over reach us, had over reached himself, wasted most of our funds, and I am not certain but that we shall after all be obliged to leave him." As for the voyagers' life in Granada, he described their amusements as "hunting, fishing and boating, and our business, studying Spanish and holding indignation meetings whenever Mr. Gordon attempted some more than ordinary outrage upon us."

Later letters informed his family they were at Leon, the capital, closer to the Pacific port of Realejo, and described the civil war engulfing the country.

On July 2 Gordon had written from Realejo to nine prominent members of the Association who were staying at Leon (they included Baldwin and his Yale companions) that the *"Sabina* had not arrived" and he had given "her up in despair." However, the *Laura Ann,* "a particularly handsome little brig said to be a fine sailor," had arrived and he had chartered her for $3,500. But, he wrote, "I cannot possibly raise this money without a loan from our people of $1,500, which must be paid on 5th July. . . She will most likely carry us to Berenica [*sic*] at the head of the Bay of San Francisco, and thus save us much danger and trouble in reaching the mines. . . The Captain and Supercargo have both recently been working in the mines, their specimens look most tempting and their report is very encouraging." Gordon was still selling the Dream!

The *Laura Ann* will also be remembered as the brig from which its captain, Lewis H. Thomas, landed in San Francisco in October 1848 and conducted services, possibly for the first time in the city according to the forms of the Episcopal Church.

Gordon's salesmanship apparently succeeded once more. On July 20, 1849, most of the company left Realejo aboard the *Laura Ann*. The *Sabina* did finally reach San Francisco just nine days after the *Laura Ann,* but carrying only 26 passengers.

Baldwin's letter from "San Francisco, Alta California," dated October 4, 1849, tells of the company's final tribulations. There were one hundred passengers on the *Laura Ann,* "a vessel of only 100 tons." (Charles Blake reported it to be 140 tons, while the newspapers stated 146 tons, neither much more adequate to its passenger load.) Baldwin wrote that much of the water had leaked from the storage tank, and a large share of the provisions had spoiled. His description paralleled George Jerome's account. The meat's smell was such that it would have sickened any but a California immigrant. They had hoped to put in at Mazatlán or San Blas for water, but a south-easter came up and bore them to Cape San Lucas. Then,

> as day after day and week after week passed by, and we were making almost no progress against the constant northwester which blew down the coast, pint after pint was knocked off our allowance, and our provisions became exhausted, one kind after another, until finally they had become reduced to bread, rice, and beans, with one quart of water a day for each man, for cooking as well as for drinking. The bread was full of worms and defiled with cockroaches; the rice was of a quality that would not bring one cent a pound in the States, half hulls, and with as many weevils as kernels. . . Like the prodigal son [I] would have been thankful enough for the mush with which grandfather's

hogs are fed, and many nights would have been glad to get my mouth into the dirtiest puddle that Chapel Street ever saw.

Finding it impossible to make San Diego, the ship was run into the shore of Lower California. There the company was fortunate; pure fresh water was found. Thirty-six hours later fortune again smiled as a Peruvian brig loaded with provisions for California anchored alongside, and food was obtained. A large number of fish were caught and salted down, and cattle were purchased. However, the supercargo, both mates, and all the sailors but two ran off. Members of the company then served as crew. Three weeks later, they entered the "magnificent bay of San Francisco."

Baldwin also related that several small parties that had broken off from the Gordon Association left Nicaragua before the *Laura Ann* sailed. One group left on a little sloop at the beginning of May, and arrived in San Francisco 144 days later, only one day before the *Laura Ann*. For 32 days they had been becalmed in one spot under a scorching sun. Their water and food became exhausted and their condition perilous. However, they made a crude still to convert salt water into drinkable water and saved their lives. Others joined a party in an iron boat from Panama, and still others fitted out a bungo at Realejo. The fate of these groups, Baldwin wrote, was unknown.

Baldwin's letter from San Francisco concluded with a description of the city: "such another city never was and never will be. Sharpers, swindlers, speculators, gamblers and rogues of every nation, clime, color, language and costume under the sun are here gathered together, and no words can convey a true idea of the result."

Colonel James I. Ayers gave a description of the

Laura Ann in his book *Reminiscences of Early California, Gold and Sunshine.* He was in Realejo when the Gordon expedition arrived, and he sailed with it on the *Laura Ann.* He characterized the ship as an "old-fashioned tub of a vessel, almost as broad at the bow as at the stern and slower than justice . . . overcrowded," with passengers "locked as close together as sardines in a box."

Baldwin's companion Charles Blake described the captain of the *Laura Ann,* Ira Blanchard, as a "shrewd, intelligent man" but "continually drunk whenever he could get liquor." Waters, the supercargo, he called "a thorough scoundrel," and Wright, the first mate, a "Texas desperado" and a "former slaver and pirate." His letter, published in March 1930, in the *Quarterly* of the Society of California Pioneers, reveals further details of the *Laura Ann's* voyage. He wrote that it landed at the mission of Todos Santos, but that neither water nor provisions could be obtained. He gave the location of the bay where water was finally found as 200 miles south of San Diego, and he identified the Peruvian ship which sold them provisions as the *Ricardo* from Callao. (It arrived in San Francisco a week after the *Laura Ann,* on October 12.)

In San Francisco, Blake encountered a Gordon Association member, George B. Hitchcock, who had left Realejo two months before the *Laura Ann,* aboard a boat only 25 feet from stem to stern. His suffering had been extraordinary. Hitchcock, who became a pioneer San Francisco bookseller and a leading stationer, later gave a statement to Hubert Howe Bancroft. He and several others had left the vessel 200 miles south of San Diego (perhaps at the same bay described by Blake) and walked up through Lower California to San Diego.

Hitchcock stated the company was delayed at San Juan, not only because of the break-down of the *Plutus'* machinery, but also because the British soldiers there were under the impression they were filibusters. Hitchcock also reported that the party in the iron boat mentioned by Baldwin finally arrived in California.

Charles Blake's letter related that the Gordons themselves had arrived in San Francisco on October 6, the day after the *Laura Ann,* on the bark *Selma.* The *Selma,* which had sailed from New York, was a 407-ton vessel, much larger than the *Laura Ann.* It is possible the *Selma* was one of the vessels referred to by Baldwin in a July 13th letter from Realejo in which he stated that there was "some prospect of our getting off," and that there were two vessels in the harbor. If so, Gordon may well have thought the larger *Selma* a safer ship for his family, and boarded her there for the voyage to San Francisco.

Neither Blake's nor Baldwin's accounts tell very much that is personal about the Gordons. However, in the diary of Samuel Linus Prindle (a film copy of which is in the Bancroft Library), a few personal remarks are found. Prindle, born in Ohio in 1823, left with the Gordon party on the *Mary.* On March 16, 1849, waiting at San Juan, he noted, "Some of the boys this evening are having their sport at the expense of Mrs. G. by playing and singing national airs in the street, because she spoke disrespectful of and refused to make an American flag." A little over a week later, a committee asked Gordon to have four or five persons associated with him speed their progress toward San Francisco, but Gordon refused. On March 28, still at San Juan, Prindle wrote "Our party is very impatient at the delay. The steamboat [*Plutus*] might have been completed in one week and here we are three, if Mr. Gordon had treated the men properly." Writing again from Granada on the shore of Lake Nicaragua on April 24: "This morn, Mr. Dale arrived [from San Juan] with the ladies which was a great relief to the mind of Mr. Gordon, who was much alarmed for their safety." Prindle also wrote how Gordon informed the company of the need of $2,250 in additional funds and on June 6, "it was agreed each man should pay $20 to secure the *Sabina.*" On June 21, when Prindle and three others engaged passage for Panama, Gordon attempted to stop them. But Prindle had arrived in California and was mining on the Mokelumne by the time he heard of the arrival of the Gordon company on the *Laura Ann.*

In 1878, William G. Doolittle, another Gordon Association member, gave a statement of his experience to Hubert Howe Bancroft. He told of meeting in Nicaragua the "negro cook, Jackson, later a celebrated cook in San Francisco." This may be William Jackson, chef of the famous restaurant, The Mint, on Commercial Street. Doolittle also made the claim that Gordon used some of the funds obtained from the Association members not only to charter the *Laura Ann* but also to buy lumber, which was "not . . . a legitimate part of the enterprise."

Samuel Smith Wood, another member of Gordon's Association, whose letters are in the Yale University Library, also expressed disapproval of Gordon. On March 18, from San Juan, he wrote to his wife, "The Gordon Association is a complete humbug. . . We have no confidence in this Mr. Gordon's Association, he is not a Gentleman and capable to conduct such men as American citizens; – he has taken us in."

Wood mined unsuccessfully in California, and returned to New York at the end of 1849. But many who sailed with Gordon on the *Mary* became well established in California. Massey and Hitchcock have been mentioned. Blake became a successful businessman, but his classmate Baldwin's life was cut short when, at the age of 31, he was thrown from a horse, resulting in his death. Joseph Britton became co-founder of Britton and Rey, the lithographers. Prindle became a Supervisor in Calaveras County; Charles Bruce Porter was elected Contra Costa assemblyman and later state senator; others earned established positions in their communities. Several settled in Tuolumne County, among them Patrick O'Byrne whose ferry service across the Stanislaus River is commemorated by the place name, O'Byrne's Ferry.

Perhaps one or another of the Tuolumne members of the Gordon Association was the source for Thomas R. Stoddard's 1861 statement that Gordon "came near being lynched by his passengers." Stoddard, a rather mysterious character who in 1850 had been responsible for the Gold Lake hoax, and later settled in Tuolumne County, was not a member of the Association.

That Gordon obtained lumber in Nicaragua is stated in John T. Doyle's manuscript. Doyle's version is that Gordon rowed out to the *Laura Ann,* which was becalmed outside Realejo, and found the ship was there to obtain lumber to take to San Francisco. After Gordon had made arrangement to charter the "tween decks" of the vessel for his passengers, he rowed ashore and visited each of the saw mills in the vicinity and contracted for all the lumber they would cut during the next thirty days. When the captain of the *Laura Ann* attempted to buy lumber he was "surprised" and "enraged" that Gordon had already bought all the available supply. However, Gordon explained to the captain that he, Gordon, was a speculator and would take the risk of the San Francisco market, while the business of the ship was that of a carrier. Further, he explained that with the pay for the freight of the load of lumber plus the charter money for the passengers, it would be a most prosperous voyage for the captain. After "some sulking" the captain agreed. "Fortune was propitious," wrote Doyle. "The lumber came to an excellent market and, on settling up accounts of the venture, Gordon found himself possessed of several thousand dollars wherewith to commence life in his new home."

Four years after the arrival of the Gordon Association, according to Doyle, Gordon invited all his old company to unite in a dinner at the Bella Union in commemoration of their journey. About a hundred attended. "After a very cordial reunion they talked of old times and old companions and adventures till long after mid-night. Gordon's little daughter Nellie, then a charming bright child of seven or eight years, was brought in by her nurse and passed round the table greeting and greeted with delight by all the guests who had petted and caressed her on the journey." The only guests who were not members of the old Association were Doyle himself and Cornelius K. Garrison, who was agent for the Nicaragua Steamship Company and Mayor of San Francisco.

As time passed, some of the discomforts of the trip were being forgotten. This is apparent in a letter Roger Baldwin wrote September 14, 1851: "My stay in lovely Nicaragua was like moments snatched from fairyland."

A number of Association reunions were held in the years to follow. In 1874, twenty-five years after the departure of the Gordon party from New York, the whereabouts of only nine members, seven residing in

San Francisco and two in Santa Clara County, were known to the reunion committee. But at the thirtieth anniversary reunion in 1879, there were eleven members from San Francisco, two from Santa Clara County and one from Oakland. Two survivors in Philadelphia sent their greetings, and others were known to be residing elsewhere in the country. According to Massey, after the death of Jerome P. Painter in 1883, the reunions ceased. Painter, who had been active in the meetings, founded the second typefoundry in San Francisco. He died as he was about to attend the February 6, 1883, dinner for the survivors of the Gordon party. Massey wrote that he himself was "finishing up the business with the caterer" when Painter's son informed him of his father's death and this "prevented any idea of festivity."

John Piersen Bering, who served as secretary for the reunions, became the last survivor. At his death on March 7, 1913, he was also the sole remaining charter member of the Society of California Pioneers. He had been successful in mining on the Yuba River, and, since 1852, had lived in San Francisco.

As noted, the Gordon Association's experiences on the way to California were similar to those of many of the parties that sailed from the Atlantic ports. Gordon's Association differed from others in having two sections, the second of which was the first organized group to attempt the Nicaragua Route. As Oscar Lewis wrote in *Sea Routes to the Gold Fields,* "The vicissitudes of Gordon's California Association seem for a time to have discouraged others from essaying this same route, and during all of 1849 the seaborne emigrants steamed on to the south, either to Panama or round the Horn." Statistics bear this out. The vast majority during the first months of the gold rush used the Cape Horn route, the number of ships using the Panama route was second, the Texas ports third, and Vera Cruz fourth. No large group except Gordon's landed at San Juan.

Gordon had claimed his section of the Association sailing on the *Mary* would reach San Francisco in sixty days. In the end it took eight long months; The *Clarissa Perkins,* carrying the first contingent of the Gordon Association had sailed all the way around the Horn and entered the Golden Gate one month earlier! Gordon's Association had "Seen the Elephant."

Gordon, the promoter, should not be too harshly criticized for the difficulties encountered by his passengers. That he expected a better voyage is indicated by the fact that he took his wife and young daughter with him on the journey. Gordon, the lumber speculator, may be more easily criticized; he apparently used the Association's money for his own benefit. However, as president and manager he may have considered himself entitled to a fee. So he arrived in the new, wild, growing San Francisco with capital to use in the mad speculation of the time!

The passengers on the two ships carrying Gordon's California Association were listed in the *New York Herald* of February 8, 1849, for the *Clarissa Perkins,* and of February 21, 1849, for the brig *Mary.* The lists are here arranged alphabetically for more convenient reference. Interestingly at least two of the passengers, Powell and Sterrett, appear on both lists, possibly either missing the first sailing or deciding to change after the first list was prepared. For the *Clarissa Perkins* the *Herald* states "Total, 127" but lists only 123 names; for the *Mary* it states "Total, 116" which appears accurate including the two ladies but not including the Gordon child. In a few cases on the first list the place of origin was shown as Gloucester, "Pa." which has been corrected to "N.J." Correction of a few names are shown in [brackets].

THE EMIGRATION TO CALIFORNIA
MOVEMENTS IN NEW YORK

Annexed is a list of passengers sailed yesterday for San Francisco in the ship Clarissa Perkins, Captain J. W. Goodrich, being part of Gordon's California Association: –

Addis, Jacob – Phila.
Anthony, Francis – New Haven
Apple, Theodore P. – Westchester, Pa.
Badger, Samuel, jun. – Phila.
Banks, E.L. – Brooklyn
Beach, E. – New Haven
Beecher, William P. – New Haven
Beers, Timothy B., M.D. – New Haven
Belrose, Thomas – Phila.
Bering, John P. – Baltimore
Bloomer, Robert – Binghampton, N.Y.
Bowers, James – Phila.
Boyd, James C. – Havre de Grace
Boyd, Samuel M. – Phila.
Brown, Henry A.B. – "
Brown, Hugh Nelson – Havre de Grace
Bryant, Alfred – Gloucester, N.J.
Burk, Isaac – Penna.
Burnham, Richard F. – Hoboken
Carver, Henry F. – Phila.
Caulk, J. Poinsett – Havre de Grace
Chamberlain, Arthur P. – Phila.
Chestnut, Benjamin – Ithaca
Cill, Alfred – Phila.

Cill, George, jun. – Phila.
Cornell, J.H. – Brooklyn
Courtney, J.F. – Havre de Grace
Cravey, Lieut. W.C. – New Haven
Crooks, Thomas, junior – Trenton, N.J.
Dana, George M. – Ithaca
Darlington, Alfred – Westchester, Pa.
Darlington, Chandler – "
Darlington, Isaac – "
Davis, George W. – Penn.
Degan, Phillip – Phila.
Dickens, Jeremiah – "
Dickey, Ellison – Paterson, N.J.
Drake, Edward P. – Ithaca
Eckley, Henry D. – "
Edgar, Edwd. J. – Havre de Grace
Engleman, Jacob – Phila.
Erskine, George – Delaware Co., Pa.
Fenn. Patrick – New Haven
Fenner, C. – "
Foster, Robert – Phila.
Foster, William B. – "
Gauze, Jesse K. – Penn.
Gegax, Samuel – Phila.
Gilbert, Owin C. – New Haven
Gilmore, David W. – Baltimore

Glass, Schenck – Havre de Grace
Gorman, Robert – Ithaca
Haines, Reuben – Phila.
Haley, William H. – "
Hall, George P. – Bridgeport
Hammond, William – Phila.
Hart, James L. –   "
Hasford, Henry A. – New York
Hazeltine, Samuel J. – Phila.
Heistand, J.C. – Phila.
Henshellwood, Archibald –
  Phila.
Hind, William L. – Ithaca
Hoffman, John Flannigan –
  Phila.
Homes, Levi – Phila.
Howell, Dr. S.W. – Phila.
Hoyt, Albert – Elizabethtown
Hunter, Charles – Flushing, L.I.
Hurlburt, Horace – New Haven
Jerome, George –   "
Johnson, David –   "
Jorden [Jarden], Samuel H. –
  Phila.
Kerk, C.H., junior – Phila.
Kimball, George W. – Water-
  town
Kintzing, Abraham M. – Phila.
Knapp, B.C. – New York
Knapp, Theodore – Putnam Co.,
  N.Y.
Laumister, George – Burlington,
  N.J.
Little, George C. – Baltimore
McAleer, James L. – York, Pa.
McCercle, William A. – Penn.
McCready, Samuel – Flushing
Marshall, Dr. Wm. –   Phila.
Massay [Massey], Atkins – "
Mayo, John – Gloucester, N.J.

Mendenhall, William S. – Penn.
Michael, Jacob O. – Havre de
  Grace
Moore, S.C. [B.C.] – New York
Moreton, James A. – Gloucester,
  N.J.
Neff, Jacob K. – Baltimore
O'Brien, James – Flushing, L.I.
O'Donnell, John – Trenton, N.J.
Osborne, Elisha C. – West Stock-
  bridge, Mass.
Painter, Jerome B. – Phila.
Payne, Robert T. – Penn.
Pennington, Joseph A. – Phila.
Powell, William – Flushing, L.I.
Rambo, George E. – Gloucester
Renaud, Alfred F. – New York
Rumsey, Charles – Penn.
Russell, William A. – New York
Sherwood, Thomas – Penn.
Shipman, C.G. – New Haven
Skeene, Augustus – Phila.
Smith, George W. – New York
Smith, J. Engal – Phila.
Smith, James Carter – Flushing,
  L.I.
Smithey, James – Gloucester, N.J.
Sneider, George – New York
Starr, Edward – Phila.
Steels, Edward –   "
Sterrett, J. Martin – Phila.
Streeper, Charles H. – "
Taylor, David – New York
Taylor, Henry F. – "
Taylor, Kendall D. – Maryland
Taylor, S. Maxwell – Pottstown,
  Pa.
Taylor, William – Gloucester,
  N.J.
Thayer, Edward – Phila.

Triebels, Francis P. – Phila.
Triebels, Peter W. –   "
Wilson, Matthew – Washington

Wintgen, John – New York
Wright, William – Havre de
Grace

List of passengers sailed [February 21] in the brig Mary, Capt. J. K. Hayes, for San Francisco, via Lake Nicaragua, as members of Gordon's California Association : –

George Gordon, President, lady and child

Adams, George
Allen, J.J. – Honesdale, Pa.
Ameridge, George – Phila.
Baldwin, Roger S. – New Haven
Baquer [Begner], A.T. –
    Pottstown
Beecher, George – New Haven
Bitting, Franklin – Reading
Blake, Charles T. – New Haven
Bowers, Wm. N. – Sullivan Co.,
    N.Y.
Bownson, Wm. – Reading
Britton, Joseph – New York
Brown, John W. – New Haven
Bruce, J.J.A. –   New York
Cardosa [Cardozo], J.N. – "
Copperthwaite, Leman – Phila.
Crittenden, A.F.
Dale, John
Deene, Charles – Reading
Dennis, Hiram
Dennison, Wm. F. – Sullivan
    Co., N.Y.
Donneghe, James C., M.D. –
    New Haven
Doolittle, H.P. – Hartford,
    Conn.
Doolittle, William G. – "
Doors, W.C., Jr. – New York
Dorr, Ezra – West Stockbridge,
    Mass.
Doughton, John – Reading, Pa.

Drury, Charles L. – Albany,
    N.Y.
Dudgeon, Enos – Reading, Pa.
Dudley, Charles P. – Chester-
    field
Dudley, William L. – "
Duncan, Henry – Belleville, N.J.
Egner, William – Phila.
Ery [Evey], ——
Evans, Dr. John F. – Pottstown
Farnham, W.H. – Bangor, Me.
Fielding, Thomas – Belleville,
    N.J.
Fisher, Aug. – Reading
Fowler, Bernard – New York
Freas, Lorenzo M. – Phila.
Gibson, George M. – Great Bar-
    ington, Mass.
Gilbert, Levi – New York
Gormon, Richard – Sullivan Co.,
    N.Y.
Greene, Henry E. – Albany,
    N.Y.
Haight, Bernardus – New York
Hall, Henry Howard – Brooklyn
Halse, A.W. – Port Jervis,
    Orange Co., N.Y.
Hardenburg, D.W. – Sullivan
    Co., N.Y.
Harrison, Joseph S.
Hawkins, Charles J. – Cayuga
    Co., N.Y.

Hawkins, M.S. – Phila.
Hayes, C.H. – Bangor, Me.
Hitchcock, George B. – New York
Hunt, D. – Phila.
Jervis, David P.
Jervis, Smith
Jolley, M.H. – Pottstown
Jordan, Robert M. – Phila.
Keyser, E. Tyson – Phila.
King, Charles M. – Germantown, Pa.
Leavenworth, Wm. C. – Reading, Pa.
Logan, H.C. – Phila.
McEwan, James D. – Ohio
McKeige, Barnett – Pottstown, Pa.
Martin, Jacob L. – New York
Martin, John L. – Pottsdam
Maupay, William A. – Phila.
Meyer, Philip –   "
Monkhouse, Col. Thomas A. – New York
Newman, J.V., M.D. – West Stockbridge, Mass.
Nicholas, Elisha – Syracuse
O'Byre [O'Byrne], Patrick – Albany, N.Y.
Pellett, Charles B. – New Haven
Perry, George F. – Sullivan Co., N.Y.
Phillips, Henry H. – New York
Porter, Charles B. – Belleville, N.J.
Potter, Charles A. – New York
Potter, Francis E. –   "
Powell, W.J. – Md.
Priesh [Priest], J.E., Engineer – Phila.

Priestly, David L.
Priestly, John W. – Phila.
Prindle, S.L. – Ohio
Reid, George W. – New York
Reilly, J. Henry – Phila.
Rogers, George W. – New York
Saurman, Abner K. – Phila.
Shofeld, David B.
Seymour, D. – Syracuse
Sherman, Wm. – Reading
Smith, F.P. – Brooklyn
Smithey, J. – Gloucester, N.J.
Snyder, Charles F. – Phila.
Soule, George – Ohio
Steadman, Charles – Phila.
Stebbins, Wm. C. – Reading
Sterret, J. Martin
Stillman, J.W. and lady – Charleston, S.C.
Stillwell, G.W. – Reading
Stratton, A.N. – Sullivan Co., N.Y.
Stuart, John – Reading
Taylor, Charles L. – Phila.
Thompson, W.H. – New York
Tooker, Dr.
Turnbull, Dalmickle – Reading
Tyler, Edwin – New Haven
Umbergield, George – New Haven
Van Riper, Peter H.
Wallace, William – Phila.
Welsh, Alfred
Wilcox, Albert – New Haven
Wood, Samuel S. – Westchester Co.
Young, Warren L. – Phila.
Young, William – Belleville, N.J.

4

The Golden Years

The Gordon California Association dissolved upon arrival in San Francisco. When, on September 12, 1849, the members of the first division arrived they found to their surprise that Gordon had not yet reached California. They did not wait for him but left at once for the gold fields. As a correspondent, "P.H.P.," wrote from San Francisco to the Boston *Herald* that same month, "all the large companies break up on their arrival here."

When Gordon arrived in October he decided that San Francisco, the bustling, hectic tent city that was growing like magic on the sand dunes, was his gold field. For the next twenty years, and especially the first few golden ones, his tireless energy and daring speculation were amazing.

The lumber he had obtained in Nicaragua found an excellent market in San Francisco. As Doyle recounted, when Gordon sold it, he "found himself possessed of a considerable cash capital."

He apparently next turned his attention to his earlier plan for a shipping line. One of his February New York *Tribune* advertisements for the Nicaragua route had stated, "This line is to be kept up in the future by the capitalists of the Association, and it is expected to prove one of the best routes to the Gold Region from the Atlantic seaboard." Also during that month, he often referred to the Association's second section as "Gordon's Passenger Line" rather than Gordon's California Association. The "capitalists" referred to were probably, in the end, only Gordon himself.

In the San Francisco *Alta California* on December 10, 1849, Gordon advertised that "the white oak ship *Clarissa Perkins,* Captain Goodrich," would be dispatched to Nicaragua with passengers bound for New York. After a ride of three days across Nicaragua, they would sail on a clipper ship up the east coast to their destination. Gordon further noted the group would be "under the guidance of A. T. Begner, interpretor and caterer and Dr. Donaghe of New Haven, physician." Dr. James Donaghe and A. T. Begner (or Beguer) had been members of Gordon's Association and apparently were planning to return home. Gordon gave his San Francisco address as "Macondray and Co., Foot of California Street." Macondray and Company was, and has been ever since, a leading shipping and trading firm in San Francisco.

Gordon's dream of establishing a regular shipping line between the eastern seaboard and California did not materialize. The control of the Nicaragua route was seized by a giant of finance, Commodore Cornelius Vanderbilt, who, by 1851, was regularly advertising his "line for California, via Nicaragua." Another notice in the *Alta* on December 26, 1849, stated the *Clarissa Perkins* would depart on January 1.

Seven months later, in July 1850, William Cathcart and Moses Leonard of San Francisco bought the ship, and the following October she was totally wrecked somewhere off the coast near Santa Cruz.

Gordon continued to be interested in chartering vessels, however, for San Francisco was the center of shipping on the Pacific Coast. He also became a wharf builder. As the city was growing with amazing rapidity, he continued dealing in lumber as well.

His shipping interests included a "fast sailing vessel"

which, according to his January 25, 1850, advertisement in the *Alta*, would be "leaving in a few days for Monterey" and returning "direct to San Francisco." A year later, he owned for a short time the 226-ton brig *Newcastle*.

Gordon's lumber interests are indicated in advertisements appearing in April 1850. They announce lumber for sale stored at the "Market Street Timber Dock" as well as "cargoes of wharf piles." He also had for sale "two powerful steam machines." He designated himself a wharf contractor and agent for the Market Street Timber Dock. This office was listed at Clay and Montgomery.

Gordon was still actively engaged in the lumber business in August. He advertised that he had "valuable Russian timber at Macondray's old yard between Sacramento and Clay on the Beach." He was also selling prefabricated buildings. Owing to the lack of facilities in California, many of the buildings were shipped in sections to be erected in place. (An example, still standing, is the Abner Phelps house, an official San Francisco landmark, which was shipped around the Horn in sections.) In September and October of 1850, Gordon had for sale a "warehouse frame" and "seven dwelling houses . . . of four to six rooms," a "one-story building, got out of Liverpool," and a church with Gothic windows that would seat 1,100. In October he advertised to the public that he would sell his stock of lumber at very low prices, as he was moving. His office was now on Leidesdorf near Sacramento Street. The rest of the year, he continued advertising lumber and prefabricated buildings, even offering a 32 room hotel on December 10.

The lumber business was booming not only because

of the tremendous building that was transforming a hamlet into the metropolis of the Pacific, but also because of numerous devastating fires. Between December 24, 1849, and June 22, 1851, six major fires laid waste to great sections of the city. Rebuilding followed quickly upon each disaster, and it is because of these early events that the city adopted the symbol of the Phoenix as part of its official seal. While some businessmen rebuilt in brick or other fire-resistant materials, there was always an immediate and great demand for lumber.

His office was now on Leidesdorf near Sacramento Street, while his lumber yard was located at the "foot of Sacramento Street." In November 1850, according to the *Alta,* he moved his lumber yard to the "foot of Taylor Street."

That the Taylor Street location was advantageous, being away from the area of the major fires, may have been one reason Gordon moved there. Another reason undoubtedly was that he had started building a wharf there for the city. The "citizens of the north part of the city" had petitioned the Town Council for this wharf, and on March 11, the Town Council had approved its construction. In October, Gordon had received the contract and started work.

The contract specified the payment of $16,000 upon completion of 100 feet of wharf. Gordon built that in six days. Instead of paying the agreed upon amount, however, the City offered him $14,000 in city scrip. Gordon chose to stop work.

City scrip, issued by the municipal government, was then selling at fifty to seventy per cent discount. San Francisco had been paying its officials monstrous salaries, grading streets, building wharves, and undertaking numerous other costly activities that had left the city with an enormous indebtedness. As the *Annals of San Francisco* explains, when the city was no longer able to pay its debts, it issued scrip, which became depreciated. Finally, in 1852, Gordon sold his $16,000 worth of rights to the contract for $2,500 to a group headed by A. Bartol, a former president of the Board of Assistant Aldermen. The newspapers stated the contract buyers intended to complete the wharf or "accept the cool little sum of $50,000." However, the Town Council refused to recognize Gordon's sale of the contract, and Alderman Harry Meiggs moved that the ordinance authorizing Gordon's construction of the Taylor Street Wharf be repealed. This was done on May 27, 1852. Nine years later, the San Francisco Chamber of Commerce reported, "The Taylor Street Wharf has long since decayed."

It appears that Gordon was not always adverse to accepting scrip, however. A newspaper item of March 11, 1851, reported he had lost his pocketbook containing $13,000 of City Wharf scrip, issued to him on February 13 of that year. The next day, the pocketbook was found and returned to him "by a member of a respectable family by the name of Lucas." To all appearances, Gordon was becoming prosperous!

The Taylor Street Wharf was not the only pier Gordon constructed. Early in 1850, he built a wharf for Henry Howison that extended from the foot of Sacramento Street, at Leidesdorf, out into the shallow Yerba Buena Cove. Howison's Wharf was extended until it finally reached 1,100 feet into the bay. At least three ships were permanently docked there and was used for storage. That it was a pier of considerable importance is indicated by the leading firms that were located there. These included Everett & Co., agents for the Empire City Line; Alfred Robinson of the Pacific Mail, Ferdinand Vassault, Bond and Hale, De Fremery and Co., and Jonathan Stevenson.

At the time of the discovery of gold in 1848, Yerba Buena Cove extended in a crescent from Clark's Point and Telegraph Hill on the north to Rincon Point and Hill on the south. Its western waters extended almost to Montgomery Street. The water was so shallow that rowboats had to be used to unload the passengers and cargoes of 1849. Thus it became advantageous and very profitable to build wharves extending into deeper water so that ships could be unloaded directly onto them. Later, these wharves were crisscrossed with streets on piles, and gradually the spaces between the piers were filled in, mostly with sand, during the period when city land was leveled and streets graded.

Gordon's association with Howison's Wharf resulted in an interesting suit in June 1850. James Blair, a steamship owner, sued Jonathan Stevenson and George Gordon, claiming that the part of the bay and harbor beyond the low water mark was a public highway and that Stevenson and Gordon had obstructed navigation by driving piles between Sacramento and Clay, off Howison's pier, thus creating a public menace. Gordon's associate in this venture was the famous Colonel Jonathan D. Stevenson who had led the First New York Volunteers (Stevenson's Regiment) to California during the Mexican War. James Blair was a member of a prominent family of public servants; his father and one brother were both Cabinet members, another brother became a United States Senator. Blair lost his case, as it was judged that Gordon and Stevensen had authority to build, and had created no public nuisance.

In 1850, new gold fields were discovered in Northern California, and ships were sailing to Trinidad Bay. At Gold Bluff, on California's coast north of Trinidad, it was reported that the black beach sand was filled with gold! In San Francisco it was "Ho! for Trinidad," and Gordon announced in the *Alta* on February 4 that the brig *Kate Heath* would sail for Umpqua and the new fields. The difficult journey to Gold Bluff by way of the Umpqua River was one recommended in misleading articles in the newspapers about the routes to these new discoveries.

Actually, the rush to Gold Bluff was a complete disappointment, as were so many future "rushes." Historian Hubert Howe Bancroft wrote that "nearly every excitement was fostered in some way by businessmen to create a demand for goods and for stage and steamer service."

The ship *Kate Heath* continued to serve Gordon. In May 1851, it was bringing him piles, and he was advertising: "The undersigned will drive piles, build foundations, erect fireproof buildings." And he was extending his scope, announcing also "wharves built up the river or down the coast."

The unsettled social conditions of San Francisco during the early 1850s are indicated in a warning of Gordon's in the *Alta* of January 8, 1851: "Notice to Timber Thieves and Wharf Rats . . . The gentlemen who are in the habit of casting adrift piles and lumber and stealing from wharves during the night are respectfully informed that if they meddle with the timber moored behind my office or remove lumber from the wharf after dark, they will be shot." In the same issue, the *Alta* commented on Gordon's notice, explaining that thieves would cast adrift the lumber, then the next day appear and claim it as salvage, while others less acquisitive would cut ropes and rejoice to see $700 or $800 worth of property drift out into the harbor on its way to the sea.

Gordon often advertised iron houses for sale. During 1852, in February he had for sale both iron fencing and "iron houses of all sizes, cheap." These prefabricated iron buildings were popular at the time. Many were shipped from England as well as from the eastern United States. For example, in September 1850, the *Diana* from Plymouth, England, which brought to California George Henry Goddard, the architect who later designed George Gordon's South Park, carried in its hold "21 packages of iron houses." So it was that, four days after the fire of June 21, 1851, the sixth of the young city's great fires, Gordon started advertising a new venture which he called "George Gordon's Block of Iron Stores." He announced "Stores and lots safe from fire . . . an entire square, bounded by Clay, Washington, Front and Davis streets." He was planning a block of uniform two-story iron buildings. In the center of the square, there was to be an 8,000-gallon water tank equipped with a hose to reach every one of the stores. Also planned was a basin by which scows could approach the rear of the stores. A day and night watchman was to be provided. Benjamin F. Butler, a well known lithographer, drew the plan of Gordon's development, showing it between the Washington Wharf and Long Wharf.

During the next few months, as Gordon attempted to sell or rent stores in this new addition to the city, he stressed its advantages: "The only effective barrier to fire is blank space and abundance of water."

Perhaps because of his new interest in the iron build-

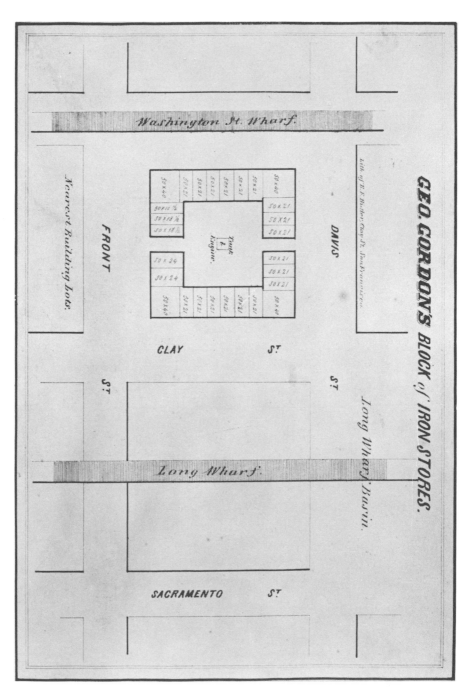

GEO. GORDON'S BLOCK of IRON STORES.

Washington St. Wharf.

Lith. of E.E. Butler, Clay St., San Francisco.

Nearest Building Lots.

FRONT

DAVIS

50 x 40 | 50 x 21
50 x 21
50 x 21
50 x 21
50 x 40

50 x 14 ½ | 50 x 21
50 x 18 ½ | 50 x 21
50 x 18 ½ | 50 x 21

Tank & Engine.

50 x 24 | 50 x 21
50 x 24 | 50 x 21
| 50 x 21

50 x 40 | 50 x 21
50 x 21
50 x 21
50 x 21
50 x 40

ST.

CLAY   ST.

ST.

Long Wharf Basin.

Long Wharf.

SACRAMENTO   ST.

A rare 1851 lithograph by Benjamin F. Butler, the first to establish a lithography plant in the new city. The print is not mentioned in Peters' *California on Stone.* Courtesy of the California Historical Society.

One Panel of a Daguerreotype of San Francisco in 1851
Gordon's Vulcan Foundry is at lower right, partially concealed by the hill.
First Street (now six blocks from the Bay!) is at lower left.
Courtesy of the California Historical Society

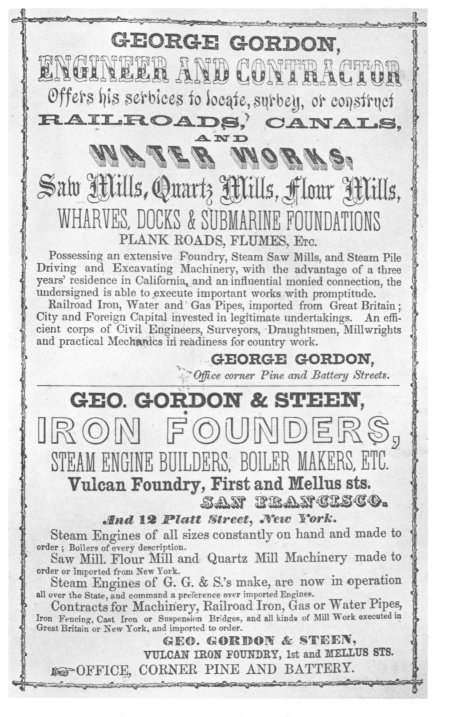

GEORGE GORDON,

ENGINEER AND CONTRACTOR

Offers his services to locate, survey, or construct

RAILROADS, CANALS,

AND

WATER WORKS,

Saw Mills, Quartz Mills, Flour Mills,

WHARVES, DOCKS & SUBMARINE FOUNDATIONS

PLANK ROADS, FLUMES, ETC.

Possessing an extensive Foundry, Steam Saw Mills, and Steam Pile Driving and Excavating Machinery, with the advantage of a three years' residence in California, and an influential monied connection, the undersigned is able to execute important works with promptitude.

Railroad Iron, Water and Gas Pipes, imported from Great Britain; City and Foreign Capital invested in legitimate undertakings. An efficient corps of Civil Engineers, Surveyors, Draughtsmen, Millwrights and practical Mechanics in readiness for country work.

GEORGE GORDON,

Office corner Pine and Battery Streets.

GEO. GORDON & STEEN,

IRON FOUNDERS,

STEAM ENGINE BUILDERS, BOILER MAKERS, ETC.

Vulcan Foundry, First and Mellus sts.

SAN FRANCISCO.

And 12 Platt Street, New York.

Steam Engines of all sizes constantly on hand and made to order ; Boilers of every description.

Saw Mill. Flour Mill and Quartz Mill Machinery made to order or imported from New York.

Steam Engines of G. G. & S.'s make, are now in operation all over the State, and command a preference over imported Engines.

Contracts for Machinery, Railroad Iron, Gas or Water Pipes, Iron Fencing, Cast Iron or Suspension Bridges, and all kinds of Mill Work executed in Great Britain or New York, and imported to order.

GEO. GORDON & STEEN,

VULCAN IRON FOUNDRY, 1st and MELLUS STS.

☞OFFICE, CORNER PINE AND BATTERY.

ADVERTISEMENTS OF GEORGE GORDON
From James M. Parker's *San Francisco Directory, 1852-53.*

ing project, Gordon's interest in the lumber business was waning in mid-1851. In June, he formed a partnership and announced his lumber business had been transferred to the firm of Gordon and Chase. Then, in October, he reported the sale of this firm because of other business pressures. In December, James Smith and Co. announced they were successors to George Gordon, and that their office was located in Gordon's Iron Block.

Gordon had changed his business. Now metal, not wood, was his main concern. He had become a partner with Edward T. Steen, an engineer and inventor, in an iron foundry and machine shop and was setting out upon a dizzying array of new activities.

On November 15, 1851, *The California Courier* noted "The Vulcan Iron Works are at last completed. They are owned by Messrs. George Gordon and Steen. The energy of these gentlemen can be shown by the fact that the whole of their premises and buildings, covering an area 100 by 700 feet, have been filled and reclaimed from flats, and put into active operation in less than six weeks since the commencement of the filling in of the lot." Early pictures show their foundry on the shore of the Bay, and call to mind that First Street was originally the first street from the Bay, thus its name.

The Vulcan Foundry Company was incorporated in 1852, and Samuel Aiken, Charles R. Steiger, and Paul Torquet were added as trustees. The capital of the corporation was $105,000. Gordon had equipped the foundry with extensive machinery purchased from B. R. Buckelew, a pioneer San Francisco newspaperman and Marin County land-owner, who had operated the California Iron and Brass Foundry.

San Francisco for many decades had important foundries, starting in 1849, with Peter Donahue's, which supplied much of the machinery for the vast mining industry of the West. Thus, as expected, the Vulcan's advertisements offered quartz mill machinery for sale. However, Gordon published a flamboyant offer headed "Investments in Quartz Mining," offering "persons wishing to invest large or small amounts in this business" a return of "8% to 20% per month." He also announced he had machinery that would test with certainty the amount of gold per ton in the quartz. Moreover, he offered his own services to determine the value of mines.

At other times during 1852, Gordon had for sale iron doors and shutters and saw mills, and he offered to construct bank vaults of brick and iron "similar to ones used by the Custom House and the banking firms of Burgoyne & Co. and that of James King of William."

The Vulcan Foundry also made threshing machines, and Gordon published the fact that the well known Bernard Murphy of San Jose had reported that his ranches "are using Gordon and Steen's threshers and they find them to work to their entire satisfaction. The straw of their barley is from 6 to 7 feet long and is found to clog up the machines manufactured in the Eastern States."

Gordon's numerous advertisements indicate his energy and the wide scope of his activity during the years 1851 and 1852. While most newspaper advertisements of that time were the same for weeks and even months, Gordon's changed almost daily. His advertisement in the San Francisco Directory of 1852-1853 is so typical of his grandiose trust in himself that it is worthy of reproduction as an illustration in this volume.

He inserted similar advertisements in other San Francisco directories of the 1850s.

Gordon continued attempting to extend his activities beyond San Francisco. In 1852, he sent to the Sacramento Common Council a plan to build waterworks for that city, and on October 25, the Council decided to submit his plan to the people. In support of his project Gordon published a statement in the Sacramento *Union* early in March 1853. He explained how he had asked for a charter to erect and operate a waterworks in Sacramento in 1852, but, as a "highly respectable and influential company" represented by Henry E. Robinson wished the same privilege, he had withdrawn and given them his plan. However, as Robinson himself had then withdrawn, Gordon had again submitted his plan. He said that he had imported water pipe from Glasgow at a very favorable price, and also had found that the citizens did not wish a private company to operate their waterworks, so he had drawn new plans and had submitted an offer to build the waterworks and then sell them to the city. He stated he would erect a three-story brick building, with pumps and steam engines, and would lay down water pipes and erect fire hydrants, in return for which the City of Sacramento would pay him $125,000 in ten-year bonds bearing an annual interest rate of 10%. Gordon listed benefits to Sacramento: filtered water, prevention of fires, reduction in the cost of water, and income to the city. He signed this statement "Geo. Gordon, engineer."

At the same time, Gordon wrote Francis W. Page of Sacramento asking the well-known banking firm of Page, Bacon and Company to finance this project if he was awarded the contract. He reminded Page that he was "a customer of your house in San Francisco."

Gordon failed to convince the voters, however. The election returns were "For Gordon's plan 452, against Gordon plan 455." So, by three votes, Gordon lost the opportunity to build Sacramento's first waterworks.

Although he had failed in Sacramento, that same spring Gordon was successful in receiving a contract from the South Fork Canal Company of Placerville. In the San Francisco *Herald* of May 7, 1853, he advertised for 50 laborers, 25 scorers and hewers, 20 quarry men and 30 carpenters to work on the construction of a 25-mile canal to carry water for mining purposes.

This contract was the source of a prolonged suit for Gordon. It was still in the courts in 1867, being at that late date in the United States Supreme Court on appeal from the U.S. Circuit Court for the Northern District of California. Gordon had stopped work on June 7, 1853, as he was not receiving payments. He sued the company and in 1854 won a large judgment, over $50,000. The company appealed this on the grounds of Gordon's failure to institute the suit before the lapse of one year, but the appeal was denied. The U.S. Circuit Court at its January 1859 term held that Gordon had a lien upon the upper section of the flume, but not the lower section which had been completed before he started work. This differed from the "court below" which held Gordon had a lien upon the entire canal. It is of interest that three of the Justices dissented, including Justice Stephen J. Field, later a member of the United States Supreme Court. The work Gordon did perform on the canal was apparently ingenious, for in 1869, at the time of his death, the *San Francisco News Letter* noted: "We may recall that the State owes to him the South Fork Canal, which he constructed in the face of difficulties which no man of less fertile resources could have overcome."

Gordon's difficulties continued that spring of 1853. On March 22, the San Francisco *Herald* reported that the day before a "part of the wharf attached to Gordon and Steen's foundry gave way to the weight of iron and coal stored on it and fell with a tremendous crash. . . Several men were engaged on the wharf and were badly injured."

Yet, with all these problems, Gordon took time to write a letter in praise of California as contrasted to Australia. Gold had been discovered in Australia in 1851. On August 20, 1852, the *Alta* had proclaimed, "But Lo a new star rises in the Pacific – California and Australia – the twin gold sisters." Many disillusioned California gold seekers sailed for the latest El Dorado. The exodus did not meet with Gordon's approval. While he never became a citizen of the United States, he was very loyal to his adopted city. On March 3, 1853, a long letter by Gordon appeared in the *Alta*. He compared wages, showing California paid twice as much as Australia, and stated "Emigration is heavy from England to Australia," and that in Australia it was a case of "work or starve." He concluded: "Save the working men the expense of an experiment . . . rather than pity them on their return disappointed and impoverished."

Gordon also entered into the Extension Bill fight. The Extension Bill was labeled "one of the great political frauds of California" by John S. Hittell in his 1878 *History of San Francisco*. It provided that the waterfront would be moved six hundred feet into San Francisco Bay beyond the line fixed by law as the permanent waterfront. Those who had acquired tentative titles to the submerged land would gain four million dollars, "which sum was to be stolen indirectly from the State

Treasury." The bill was sponsored in the State legislature by David C. Broderick, then a state senator. Both he and his friends owned titles that would be confirmed by this bill. These were titles to water lots obtained during the Peter Smith land sale, which many had considered illegal. Gordon may have been one of the first to realize the dangers of the Extension Bill. The *Herald,* on February 7, published a letter signed "Vulcan," written in Gordon's style. With sarcasm he criticized Governor John Bigler's effort to impose the Extension Bill on San Francisco.

The *Herald* was the city's leading newspaper. It editorially denounced the Extension Bill as "knavery." When the bill passed the Assembly, it proclaimed: "The first of April 1853 will be memorable in the annals of California as a day of national humiliation and disgrace." All of San Francisco's assemblymen not only voted against the bill but also resigned from the legislature. On April 13, there was an Anti-Extension mass meeting at the Merchants Exchange, called for the purpose of defeating the bill in the Senate. Urging its defeat was George Gordon, joined by such civic leaders as William T. Coleman, Colonel Edward Baker, H. H. Haight and James Donahue. Both the *Herald* and the *Alta* published Gordon's letter urging the people to re-elect the resigned assemblymen. This they did. At a special election, San Francisco returned them by a five-to-one vote.

The Extension Bill was defeated in the Senate only when the chairman, Lieutenant-Governor Samuel Purdy, voted, breaking a tie. As a consequence, Broderick blocked Purdy's nomination as the Democratic candidate for governor. Instead, Bigler received the nomination and was re-elected by a very close vote. He

was believed to have been aided by Broderick's ballot-
stuffing cohorts.

Another problem caused conflict in San Francisco.
The grading of streets necessitated the raising of buildings in certain cases. On September 29, 1853, Milo
Hoadley was appointed Civil Engineer for San Francisco. The previous August, he had submitted a report
regarding the city's grades. He had conceived a plan
which called for the leveling of Telegraph Hill and
other hills, leaving the city flat and thus in his opinion
more easily developed. During February and March,
many articles appeared in the newspapers attacking this
plan. For example, Beck and Elam, commission merchants located on Jackson Street between Sansome and
Montgomery, wrote that their 50 by 80 foot building
would have to be raised; that Gordon and Steen esti-
mated the cost at $7,000, and that their total loss would
be $25,000. On April 3, 1854, the Common Council
decided that because of "sufficient manifestations of
disapproval on the part of the people," engineers
should be employed to investigate. Those selected were
J. G. Barnard, Brevet Major, U.S. Corps Engineers;
A. T. Arrowsmith, Civil Engineer; and J. A. Hardie,
First Lieutenant, Third Artillery. On May 10, they
submitted their findings, which were most critical of
the Hoadley plan. They claimed millions would be
spent to destroy the natural advantages of the hills, and
urged that, as they were not nuisances, the hills should
be preserved. They also called for the creation of more
parks. Hoadley replied on May 22, again urging the
leveling of the hills. He also said that in preparing his
original report he had been aided by William P. Hum-
phreys and J. H. Hubbell, civil engineers. By the time
the Common Council finally took action on July 7, 1854,

Hoadley's report had been greatly modified, and the hills were saved.

On this subject Gordon took no public stand, but during the period of controversy he did not fail to have notices in the newspapers advertising his equipment for raising buildings. Although in the end hills were not leveled, street grading that necessitated the moving of buildings was done. Apparently Steen had developed the first patented equipment for raising houses. In September 1853, the *Herald* told of Gordon and Steen's "machinery capable of lifting 4,000 to 5,000 tons, and quite able to elevate brick buildings below the newly established grades." The *Herald* on February 8, 1854, under the caption "Raising Houses" noted "the Hydraulic Press for raising houses, invented and manufactured by Messrs. Geo. Gordon and Stein [*sic*] of the Vulcan Iron Works, is now being used with great success. An example was given of one structure that had been lifted successfully, that of George Clifford and Company's brick building, on Clay near Montgomery.

On September 12, 1852, a letter to the editor of the San Francisco *Herald* inquired if salt water (sea water) could be used in making bricks. The editor stated the question was important, probably reflecting the city's concern over a lack of an adequate water supply, and asked for a reply from a "scientific friend." The following day Gordon replied, claiming that salt water could be used if the bricks were burnt correctly. He also advised that salt would damage sun-dried bricks, such as adobes. As salt attracts moisture, it is doubtful that many followed Gordon's idea.

Gordon continued his interest in other public affairs of his city. On March 11, 1854, he had a long letter published in the *Herald*. It was addressed to the Common Council and was critical of that body's methods of maintaining the streets. He urged asphalt pavements or "McAdamized" roads rather than the planked surfaces that had been used. For sewers, he advised redwood rather than Oregon pine, the use of which he called an "injudicious expenditure." In conclusion, he called for the Council to seek the advice of "mechanics, architects, engineers and contractors" in an effort to solve the street problems.

In 1854, Gordon had personal difficulties that were recorded in the newspapers. On February 15, the *Herald* reported, "Shooting. On Dupont near California. Mr. James George is erecting a building on a lot adjoining the house of George Gordon. The eaves on one side of this latter house project over the lot on which Mr. George is building and interfere with the construction of the new tenement. . . Yesterday Mr. George was engaged in cutting it away, when Mr. Gordon came out of his house with a pistol in his hand and forbade the proceedings, whereupon the latter took up a gun that he had at hand and fired at Gordon. Some of the shot passed through the latter gentleman's hat, but did not hit his body. The affair ended there, and Mr. George has been arrested on complaint of Mr. Gordon for assault with a deadly weapon." Six days later the *Herald* reported that "The Recorder observed that after careful examination of the facts he could not be justified in discharging the accused," and bail was set at $1,500.00.

This house of Gordon's was undoubtedly his residence on Dupont Street. In 1850 he had lived at Washington and Virginia streets (the latter, between Stockton and Powell, now Trenton), but by 1852 he had moved to Dupont (now Grant Avenue). It must have been a pleasant residence. Six years after he had moved to South Park, when he offered it for sale in 1861, he described it in an advertisement: "Home and garden lot . . . near the center of the City . . . eligible family residence on Dupont Street, opposite St. Mary's Cathedral . . . surrounded by a brick wall containing a conservatory, fruit trees."

A more tragic event than the shooting which indirectly involved Gordon occurred in the spring of that year. On April 15, the steamboat *Secretary* exploded near the mouth of Petaluma Creek. More than sixteen people were killed including Major John Ebbetts, whose name is memorialized by Ebbetts Pass in the Sierra Nevada. The *Secretary* had been racing the *Nevada* when the accident occurred. Gordon and Steen were not only part owners of the *Secretary* but the Vulcan Foundry had re-built its boiler. Its engine was the same that had been used on the ill-fated *Sagamore,* a steamboat that had blown up as it left San Francisco for Stockton on October 29, 1850, leaving fifty dead.

The Grand Jury on June 3, 1854, accused Gordon and Steen of "culpable negligence" in the matter of the explosion of the *Secretary*. Numerous suits against the partners followed the accident but none was successful. For example Davis vs. Gordon and Steen resulted in a verdict of "not fully sustained." The case of Snyder vs. Gordon and Steen ended when the jury was not able to come to a decision. In Lewis vs. Gordon and Steen, Lewis asked damages for the loss of an eye and right arm and for leg injuries. John T. Doyle, defending Gordon, claimed criminal negligence on the part of Lewis, who was on the steamer to repair machinery. Lewis did not win his case.

Jerry MacMullen states in his *Paddlewheel Days in*

California that during the inquest, it came out that the *Secretary's* engineer had actually brought about the explosion by holding down the safety valve with an oar until the boiler could stand no more pressure.

The Vulcan Foundry continued to build boilers. In August 1885, it installed a new boiler in the ship *Helen Hensley*. This time Gordon demonstrated caution, announcing that the United States inspector of boilers, George Coffee, had tested the boiler and found it worthy.

In spite of all the trials, Gordon continued to write letters to the newspapers. On August 7, 1854, his letter entitled "The Way the City Does Business" appeared in the *Alta*. He stated he had bid $23,000 to erect a fence around Portsmouth Plaza which had been allowed to deteriorate disgracefully. Conjointly with his firm, Babcock and Smart offered to grade the Plaza for $6,250, making a total of $29,250. Nevertheless, Nutting and Zottman's bid of $33,000 won them the contract.

Further, Gordon wrote, the Council wished to open Davis Street between Pacific and Broadway, and a firm with which he was associated, James Smith and Company, wharf builders, had bid $5,450 cash, or warrants to the sum of $6,808. Roberts and Company were awarded the contract although their bid was $6,800 cash. (Gordon had apparently kept an interest in his contractor's firm after he had sold it to Smith and Company.)

Gordon concluded his letter by stating that he had not written as a "disgruntled person" but to "extol the Council for its munificence."

At this time, Harry Meiggs represented the First Ward on the Board of Aldermen, and served on the

committee on streets and public buildings. After
George Gordon had abandoned the building of the
Taylor Street Wharf, Meiggs, who was also in the
lumber business in North Beach, built nearby his famous Meiggs Wharf. According to legend, Meiggs and
Gordon had a scheme to develop Telegraph Hill, but
the events of 1854 indicate that if there had been a
business association, it was over by then, for Gordon
was indeed critical of Alderman Meiggs' actions. This
was in the period when Harry Meiggs was becoming
desperate because of lack of funds.

Meiggs, through his lumber activities, including saw-
mills in Mendocino County, had become one of the
wealthiest men of San Francisco. He believed that the
future of San Francisco lay in the level area of North
Beach, and he invested heavily in large sections of land
there. However, city growth turned southward and his
speculation failed. In an attempt to avoid disaster
"Honest Harry," as he was known, forged city war-
rants. Finally to avoid debts of hundreds of thousands
of dollars, he sailed out through the Golden Gate, but
not into obscurity. In South America, as a builder of
railroads in Chile and later Peru, he became, as one
biographer has called him, "Yankee Pizarro." But he
was never able to return to the land of his birth.

Bancroft, in his *California Inter Pocula,* wrote that
there could be no doubt that Meiggs, "the arch-crim-
inal, had confederates in the Board of Aldermen, of
which he was shortly before a member, [and] among
the street contractors, of whom he was a special patron."
One might conclude that there was some substance to
Gordon's letter to the public.

With all his activities of 1854, Gordon maintained
his interest in the Vulcan Foundry. Among his distin-

guished clients was John Bidwell, "Prince of California Pioneers" as Rockwell D. Hunt so aptly called him. He ordered iron machinery from the Vulcan Foundry for his great Chico Ranch in the Sacramento Valley. In the California State Library are letters and receipts from the Foundry addressed to "Major John Bidwell" (he had yet to be addressed as General!). The shipments were to "Bidwell Landing," located at the confluence of Big Chico Creek and the Sacramento River. The machinery was shipped on the Sacramento River boat *Confidence,* and payment was to be deposited with the banking firm of Drexel, Sather and Church.

During this same year the Vulcan Foundry moved its office from the corner of Pine and Battery to the corner of Montgomery and Commercial.

The Golden Years of San Francisco were about to close; but George Gordon was developing yet another project, one for which he is best remembered; the creation of South Park, the city's first planned residential area for the elite.

5

South Park and the 'Fifties

Early in 1852, George Gordon had begun to buy property in San Francisco outside the business district, in what was still considered a suburban area. Most of his purchases were south of Market Street. By 1854 he had acquired some twelve acres on the south side of Rincon Hill, and that year he issued an eight-page prospectus for a fine new residential development that he had named "South Park." It was intended to rival in elegance the private residential parks of London and New York.

One of the first lots he acquired was purchased from James Blair, the same James Blair who had sued Gordon and Colonel Stevenson in 1850. It was lot number 87 at the northwest corner of Second and Bryant streets, just across Bryant from South Park proper. His problems with it were typical of the problems of almost all land buyers in San Francisco in those unsettled years. To clear the title, Gordon had to make small payments to two claimants, Joseph Wilson and Martin Waterman in 1852, and the following year, another payment to Captain John Farren. Also in 1853, Gordon later recalled, "Judge Nathaniel Bennett, but recently Chief Justice of the Supreme Court of California, squatted upon lot No. 87." This action, Gordon added, resulted in three years of litigation and cost him $6,700.

There were other claims to lot 87 as well. The *Alta* of January 12, 1855, reported "an action in ejectment" in the Twelfth District Court, brought by George Gordon against John T. Brown, apparently another squatter. The verdict, reported the next day, was in favor of Gordon.

Although the San Francisco *Elite Directory* of 1879 states that George Gordon had purchased the land of South Park from Squire P. Dewey, the well known real estate auctioneer, Dewey actually acted only as an agent and notary for Gordon. The records in San Francisco City Hall confirm Gordon's statements that he bought the property piecemeal, the major seller being James Blair.

South Park itself consisted of six 100-vara lots which, after purchasing them, Gordon subdivided into homesites. In 1860, while testifying in the Rodman Price case, he claimed he had paid $3,000 for lot 94, at the southwest corner of Bryant and Second, and $5,000 each for lots 95 and 105, which formed the center of South Park. Lots 96 and 104, the section bordering Third Street, cost $6,500 each. Lot 106, consisting of the southeast section, cost $22,500 according to Gordon. Records in a later case indicate that the amount paid by Gordon for lot 106 was only $18,000 but, as noted later, he may have added in other costs. In any case, he stated that lot 106 had "no more intrinsic value than those for which I paid only three and five thousand dollars." Taking Gordon's own figures, the six South Park parcels cost him a total of $48,500. Three lots across Bryant Street, which were not in South Park proper but which Gordon bought and included in the prospectus, were the troublesome lot 87, lot 86, and lot 85. Gordon stated he had paid $2,700 for lot 87, and $1,600 for one half of lot 86.

South Park was bounded by Second, Third, Bryant and Brannan streets. It was described by the 1856 San

Francisco Directory as "the only level spot of equal area, free from sand, within the city limits." The directory noted that "one-fourth of the lots – being a quarter section of the improvement – were built upon by Mr. Gordon in 1854. . . The cost of this block of buildings was $110,000. . . From the basement of each lot clay was taken sufficient to make bricks for the houses erected thereon. . . Water is obtained at the depth of 25 feet. . . The building provisions give almost perfect security against fire."

Gordon's eight-page "Prospectus of South Park," printed by Whitton, Towne and Co. in San Francisco in 1854, is now an exceedingly rare pamphlet. In it Gordon explained the plan of South Park. There were sixty-eight building lots "of twenty-two to twenty-nine feet frontage" (actually some had a twenty-one foot frontage), with depths varying from 97 to 137½ feet. He explained that his object was to lay out "ornamental grounds and building lots on the plan of the London Squares, Ovals or Crescents, or of St. John's Park or Union Square in New York, and equally elegant."

Controls were to be exercised, "all stores or workshops, saloons, etc. being strictly prohibited and houses must be of brick or stone and occupied exclusively for private dwellings." (The fact is that all of the early houses in South Park were built of brick, covered with a stucco that gave the appearance of stone.) "The architectural designs of South Park have been made by George H. Goddard Esq. late architect to Lord Holland, and who laid out that magnificent addition to the West End of London, known as the Holland Park Estate."

Goddard himself described his work on South Park in a letter of April 30, 1854, to his brother Augustine.

"I have got a job of laying out a large plot of ground for a square and ornamental garden with houses round for Villa residences a mile out of San Francisco, something in the mode of the new parts around London. My view of Lord Holland's Estate, Addison Gardens, procured me this work."

The houses themselves were described in an 1860 pamphlet of John Middleton and Son, one of Gordon's later real estate auctioneers. Most were two stories with an English basement. One exception was Archibald A. Ritchie's three story residence, located on the northwest corner of South Park and Center Street. Center Street divided the crescents into east and west sections. The northwest section was the first to be built upon.

The floor plans of all the houses were similar. The basement of each contained the dining rooms, kitchen, servants' rooms and pantries. On the first floor were the parlors, and on the second floor were the bedrooms, usually five. In a separate building, at the rear, were the stables and the coachman's quarters.

Tradesmen's deliveries were made by way of small streets, then known as Park Lane North and Park Lane South, that ran along the back of each property. The stables were also reached by these lanes. Park Lane North is now Taber Place, and Park Lane South is Varney Street.

The oval garden in the center of South Park was described in the San Francisco Directory of 1856: "75 feet wide and 550 feet long . . . laid out down the center of the block, surrounded by an ornamental iron railing."

There are two persistent legends regarding this garden. One is that its shape and size were exactly the same as those of the famed *Great Eastern* steamship, the largest vessel in the world of its time. Idwal Jones, for example, writing in the San Francisco *Examiner* of 1924, stated Gordon "secured plans of the ship . . . and pored over them. Then he pegged out the park to the exact dimensions." However, the facts are that construction of the *Great Eastern* was not started until 1854 and its dimensions were 693 feet in length and 83 feet in breadth, somewhat larger than South Park.

The other legend has the South Park garden as an exact copy of Berkeley Square in London. This is also untrue, as is apparent to anyone who has seen both. Size and dimensions differ. Berkeley Square is 2.46 acres, while South Park is only three quarters of an acre.

By the end of 1854, South Park was visibly taking shape. On December 25 the *Alta* reported: "We visited this handsome addition to the beauty and convenience of our city a day or two since and are very pleased with the progress of the improvements. We doubted somewhat when the program came out some three months ago whether the enterprising project would meet support in these dull times, but South Park is now a fixed fact. Seventeen stately residences are already constructed. The central part or park is enclosed in an exceedingly elegant iron fence. . . The grounds are tastefully laid out, already about 1,000 young trees and shrubs are planted. . . Safe from fire, South Park we think must become a choice place for residence."

Gordon's first newspaper advertisements for South Park appeared in January 1855. They announced a "Great Sale" of 32 building lots facing the oval park, to be held on January 30 by Theodore Payne, a leading real estate auctioneer of the 1850s. Terms were "one-third cash, the balance in six and twelve months, at

2 percent per month." The *Alta* noted that the seventeen houses which had been built faced south in the northwest quarter. The *Weekly Chronicle* of January 27, 1855, gave their total cost as $150,000.

A few days after the sale the *Daily Herald* had an editorial titled "Ornamenting the City – South Park." It stated that in spite of pressure of hard times, there were noticeable improvements taking place in the "suburbs" of San Francisco:

"To George Gordon the city is indebted for one of the handsomest and most extensive improvements made during the past year. We allude to the laying out and ornamenting of South Park and erection of seventeen elegant brick dwelling houses facing it." The article later alluded to the houses as mansions and also noted that "Third Street has been opened through the sand hills."

Gordon did not sell all the lots that he offered at the January 20 auction. He continued to advertise the remainder through the year. The fact that sales were slow was due partially to the depression that gradually developed in 1854 and climaxed in 1855. The placer mines were yielding decreasing amounts of gold and many miners drifted back to San Francisco to join the unemployed. This decline in gold production led to the end of flush times. The golden years had fostered over-speculation; now failures occurred, like that of Harry Meiggs in October 1854. In February 1855, the great banking house of Page, Bacon and Company suspended operations. This was followed by the closing of Adams and Company, the largest express company in the state. The panic spread and many leading banks closed. As the *Herald* had noted, South Park was indeed launched during difficult financial times.

VIEW OF SOUTH PARK FROM THIRD STREET

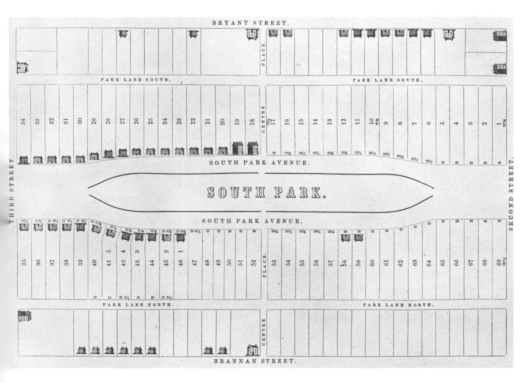

SOUTH PARK ON SAN FRANCISCO'S RINCON HILL
The view is architect Goddard's 1854 drawing, lithographed by Britton & Rey.
The plat is from John Middleton's "Auction Sale of Real Estate, October 22, 1860,"
of five houses on the south side, and seventeen lots.
Both items from the author's collection.

But gradually lots were sold, and South Park and nearby Rincon Hill became "social centers" as the city's *Elite Directory* of 1879 designated them. "There was little that was stylish or correct in the city except in its vicinity," it noted. As numerous articles and books describing San Francisco have stated, South Park was the center of fashion and the dwelling place of the elite during the 1850s and 1860s. Not until the Second Street cut of 1869 changed the character of the area and the invention of the cable car in 1873 allowed easy access to Nob Hill did the gradual flight of fashionable South Park dwellers occur.

In the 1850s, many prominent San Franciscans became South Park residents. Among them were Robert B. Woodward, who later developed Woodward's Gardens; Isaac Friedlander, the grain king; John Redington, wholesale druggist; Lloyd Tevis, later president of Wells Fargo and Company; Charles De Ro, auctioneer and later president of Gordon's sugar company; George Johnson, importer of iron and steel, and consul for Norway and Sweden; James Otis, later mayor of San Francisco; William M. Lent, wealthy mining man; David Colton, the attorney who was later associated with the "Big Four" railroad builders; and the Rev. William A. Scott, the Presbyterian minister who established Calvary Church and later St. John's Church in San Francisco.

Other well known men who resided in South Park in the 1860s included Senator William M. Gwin; Isaac Davis, the lime and cement dealer, later a partner with Cowell; General Barton S. Alexander; General Rene De Russey; Dr. Richard Ashe; Dr. Beverly Cole, one of the few Californians to be elected president of the American Medical Association (1896); Commodore

James T. Watkins of the Pacific Mail Steamship Company; Gregory Yale, a mining attorney; Celedonio Ortiz, a Spanish capitalist; Charles Lux of the Miller and Lux cattle empire; Asa P. Stanford, brother of Leland Stanford; and Elisha W. McKinstry, Justice of the Supreme Court of California; and many other residents prominent in the building of San Francisco.

With all the space available in the still not heavily populated city, one might wonder why so many of the elite chose these homes which were built close together, with small frontages. Gordon gave important reasons: South Park was a residential area free of saloons, gambling halls and other undesirable neighbors. It was safe from fire; the houses, built of brick, away from the flimsy wooden dwellings of the gold rush city, were well protected against burning. As already mentioned, San Francisco had been destroyed six times by fire.

An example of the city's lack of zoning protection was Pike Street in what is now Chinatown. This street had been given to the city by Dr. Augustus J. Bowie, whose property and house were situated in that block in the early 1850s. It was named in honor of his wife, a member of a well known Maryland family. When the street became notorious because of its numerous brothels, the Bowies moved away, and Pike Street's name was changed to the more poetic Waverly Place, in a vain attempt to return the area to greater respectability.

Besides the reasons advanced by Gordon for the desirability of residing in South Park, another factor is suggested by Gunther Barth of the University of California in his essay "Metropolism and Urban Elites in the Far West." He wrote: "Its very compactness, with houses crowded together on twenty-five foot frontages, gave the residents a physical metropolism amid the sprawling sand dunes that obscured the rest of the city."

Between 1860 and 1864, George Gordon made great efforts to sell the remainder of his South Park property. He very probably had become tired of the project and realized it was not likely to bring him wealth. He also needed capital for his expanding sugar refinery, and for the expenses of a country estate, for he had begun purchasing land south of San Francisco on which to build a pretentious new residence.

During 1860 he placed advertisements in the San Francisco newspapers, including the foreign language papers, offering for sale one completed and six unfinished houses in South Park. He also had for sale a corner lot at Davis and Commercial Streets and another corner lot at Taylor and Vallejo which he described as "not very accessible at present, but commanding a magnificent view." His offices were listed at the refinery and on Sansome Street.

In October 1860, John Middleton, the well known auctioneer, was advertising six unfinished brick houses in the southwest quarter of South Park for sale. Middleton also had a pamphlet printed announcing the auction sale of real estate on October 22, 1860. Many parcels are described. South Park property included five unfinished houses and seventeen lots in the northeast quarter. In the pamphlet is a "pull-out" map of South Park showing the location of all the dwellings erected there at that time. Construction of new houses for sale had been reported earlier in the year. On January 7 the *Bulletin,* in describing "Progress of Permanent Improvements in San Francisco during 1859," stated: "There has been a revival of work of improvement of South Park which has become one of the most desirable locations in the City."

In October 1861, a year later, the *Bulletin* reported that Gordon had built "English basement houses" in the northeast quarter section of South Park. The article also related that "10 residences built at once can be erected cheaper than single improvers can hope to build," and further that "Mr. Gordon has arranged, we hear, with a company of Eastern mechanics whom the war has thrown out of work [to come to San Francisco] at wages but a little over Eastern prices," and that he had advanced their passage money. Whether this ambitious arrangement was actually carried out is not known.

The "English basement houses" were described in the *San Francisco News Letter* on December 26, 1861: "ground floor: vestibule, and entrance hall, library, two servants' rooms, kitchen, two storerooms, wine cellar, fuel room etc.; on main floor: drawing room, conservatory, parlor, and dining room; the chamber floor: five bedrooms, closets, bathroom and water closet." Gordon's address was now given as 411 Merchant, near Battery.

In the same issue of the weekly circular, Gordon had for sale sixteen lots in South Park. As added inducements, he offered plans and drawings for buildings to be erected on them. He also offered to supply the labor of "masons, carpenters, plasterers, painters and plumbers" and advertised "mantles, grates, plate glass, imported from New York" for sale at cost, and "Loans made [on] 90 percent of value."

The *Alta* commented that the location was "not only eligible and healthful for private residences, but has unobstructed views of the Bay, Alameda, the City and its surroundings" and that "these lots are located in one of the most pleasant neighborhoods in the city, surrounded by elegant improvements and fronting a beautiful garden, which is kept constantly in fine condition." However, Gordon was still advertising the 16 lots in June, and some apparently remained unsold in September.

In March 1863 Gordon was advertising lots for sale on Second Street "overlooking the Bay and Contra Costa" and explaining: "The owner of the property requiring funds for manufacturing purposes, will close out at low prices, as low as building lots on the sand-filled swamp west of 3rd Street are selling for."

Finally, in April 1864, the "Great Closing Sale of the South Park Property by Order of George Gordon Esq." was announced by Jerome Rice, auctioneer. Now added to the inducements was "the proximity of the property to the San Jose railroad," which had just been constructed. In July 1864, through the *News Letter,* Gordon offered lots on Second and Brannan Streets, and again stated he required "funds for manufacturing purposes."

The South Park project, ambitious as it was, did not engage the entire attention of vigorous George Gordon. It was his opinion that the business depression of San Francisco could be alleviated by an increase in the city's population. Many of San Francisco's prominent men held this same belief, and organizations were formed to promote emigration from other parts of the nation and the world. Gordon was a member of the executive committee of the Pacific Emigrant Society and later secretary of the Immigrant Association.

On February 10, 1855, the *Weekly Chronicle* printed a letter of George Gordon addressed to the State Emigration Society. It commenced, "The workmen of the Vulcan Iron Foundry beg to submit. . ." Gordon suggested that the state should undertake management of immigrant ships, some "steamships known as propellers" and "some clipper ships equipped with engines," the trip to be at reasonable cost.

On June 23, Gordon addressed the people in the same newspaper. He stated he had "no private ends to serve, no profit to gain" but that he "owes to California six years of pleasant residence and what worldly gain I have, and this is my apology if one is needed for making these suggestions." He called for 20,000 more residents to enter California. The *Chronicle* referred editorially to Gordon's communication as the "noble letter of Mr. Gordon" and stated that the "plan of Mr. Gordon is good, very good."

Gordon's letter elicited a number of replies, some quite critical. One writer, signing himself "A Naturalized Citizen," gave several objections. He wrote that first the squatters, the land grabbers, must be controlled, and also, if a large number of people arrived, there might not be enough jobs. Further, he stated that foreigners must receive better treatment in America than they were receiving, and lastly that the owners of lots were the ones who wished for more people in California.

Gordon, as usual, replied quickly with a rejoinder: "Being a foreigner myself, with a residence of ten or twelve years in the United States, I cannot remember a single act of discourtesy to me because of my nationality. . . Foreigners do not come to America to be Judges, Mayors, Aldermen – they come to America to make a living by pursuit of their business. It is our duty and to our interest to avoid those topics which provoke these asperities."

Another letter critical of Gordon's plans stated, "Foreigners land and three days later become naturalized and get in on the spoils." This letter possibly reflects the Know-Nothing spirit of the times, and the anti-Irish sentiment which evidenced itself strongly a year later during the period of the Second Vigilance Committee. Other letters objecting to population expansion pointed out that it would lead to a "cheaping of labor," and prophesied that "notorious speculators in real estate will not succeed" in their plans for increased immigration.

While Gordon did not reply to the charge that lot owners had a special interest in immigration, he, in effect, confirmed it in a later letter stating that additional residents aid the landowners, those with "To Let" signs on their buildings and those with empty lots. He told how, in 1854, the tide of prosperity had ebbed, Chinese immigration had stopped owing to "calamitous legislation," wages were reduced, and real estate values, rents and interest rates declined. These conditions, he wrote, continued in 1855, and as for 1856, "Quien sabe?"

In his capacity as secretary of the Immigration Association, Gordon called a meeting for July 24 and addressed it. To quote the July 25 *Alta,* "he brought down the house with repeated rounds of applause when he proposed consideration of a line of vessels exclusively for the transportation of female passengers to California." In this, Gordon was reflecting the general view held during the 1850s, when all deplored the scarcity of women in California.

In a letter to the *Alta* on July 26, 1855, "Civis" called Gordon's proposal "absurd," stating that if Eliza Farnham could not accomplish the mission of bringing moral women to California, no one could. The reference was to Mrs. Farnham's abortive effort in 1850 to bring unmarried women from New York in an effort to up-grade the moral life of San Francisco.

Another "liberated" woman of that era was Emily Edwards who presided over the Half Way House on the north side of Folsom Street between Tenth and Eleventh Streets. The *Alta* on May 17, 1855, described her as one who defied a marshal over a land controversy, caught an attempted murderer, dashed into a smoking ruin and rescued a stricken fireman, and two years previously aided Mr. Gordon when his horse had become mired in a bog at Folsom and Johnson (now 9th) Streets and would have perished had not the doughty Emily "pitched into the mud" and got the horse out while a "crowd of lookers on of the sterner sex had 'give him up.'" Gordon rewarded her with gifts including a new dress.

Gordon wrote a series of articles regarding immigration for the San Francisco *Weekly Chronicle*. One, published October 13, 1855, urged Californians to stay in their state and not to follow the "erratic Walker comet." William Walker, the "Grey-eyed Man of Destiny," had that spring led a group of California filibusters in an amazing attempt to conquer Nicaragua and all of Central America. Gordon's article attacked the motives of Walker's band and the conditions in Nicaragua as well. By coincidence, the author's copy of Walker's *The War in Nicaragua* is inscribed by Walker himself to Gordon's attorney and friend, John T. Doyle. In the book is a note by Doyle which reads: "I became acquainted with General William Walker in San Francisco. . . We dined usually at the same restaurant, and frequently at the same table. . . In New York . . . he came to lodge in the same house where I had rooms

. . . most of his evenings were passed in my parlour, where we regularly dined together and where he wrote his history, *The War in Nicaragua."* The book was inscribed to Doyle on March 19, 1860, less than seven months before the day, September 12, that Walker met his death before a firing squad in Honduras.

Gordon wrote of the advantages of living in California in contrast to Nicaragua, recalling his own experiences en route to California: "We were the first and foremost of the long caravan which has since wended its way to California via Nicaragua."

He related incidents of the trip and life in that country, including costs in 1849: "the messes $1.00 per day for ten persons." Gordon's long letter concluded with a warning to the filibusters that they would return to California "enfeebled, attenuated, with the seeds of complex diseases deeply seated in your frames . . . with scarcely strength sufficient left to lean against a bar and ask for a morning cocktail."

On November 10, shortly after writing this article, Gordon addressed the Immigration Association at the Music Hall. According to the *Herald,* he urged the "dissemination, in a popular manner, of statistical information of California," a reduction in "the rate of passage" and "employment for immigrants immediately on their arrival." Further, he suggested that a weekly newspaper be published in New York "for the dissemination of California intelligence," distribution of 250,000 copies of a pamphlet to be printed about California, and the publication of a book about the state. Lastly, he asked for the establishment of information offices throughout the country with Wells Fargo and Company acting as agents.

Meanwhile, Gordon continued to be active in the

Vulcan Foundry, and it was from that address, on December 16, 1855, that he wrote to Henry W. Halleck who was administering the property of the late Captain Joseph L. Folsom, whose large land holdings were soon to be sold at auction. Gordon's letter contained advice regarding the sale. He suggested posters be circulated "through the mines – say in the thousands – calling attention to this property." It was his belief that miners did not read the regular San Francisco real estate advertisements and were "burying their money from lack of confidence," but would realize the "prospect of advance in value," and would be attracted in "large numbers" to buy land. Gordon concluded: "Excuse the suggestion if you don't like it."

As mentioned, a difficulty in owning land in early San Francisco was obtaining clear title. One of Gordon's particularly lengthy suits concerned South Park lot 106 at the northwest corner of Second and Brannan. This was the lot he said he bought for $22,500; and perhaps he added to the original price the interest on the mortgage and the costs of litigation.

It had been owned by Dr. John Townsend. Dr. Townsend died of cholera on December 8, 1850, and his wife died two days later from the same disease. Their infant, John Henry Townsend, was their heir, and his uncle, Moses Schallenberger, was appointed guardian. One of the appraisers of the estate was Talbot Green. The property was sold on February 2, 1852, for $634.00 to Michael Reese, who bought most of the Townsend estate. Reese, known to his contemporaries as "the meanest man in San Francisco," then conveyed all of the San Francisco property except lot 106 to Elisha O. Crosby, who was serving as attorney for the Townsend estate at the time of the sale. When this arrangement was later alleged to be fraudulent, doubt was thrown on the legality of Gordon's purchase. Reese sold lot 106 to Gordon for $18,000 on August 14, 1854 (for a profit of $17,366 in two years), and Gordon gave Reese a mortgage on the property.

In 1861, Samuel J. Hensley, who had succeeded Schallenberger as guardian of young Townsend, sued Gordon claiming Schallenberger had sold lot 106 illegally. The State Supreme Court upheld him and ruled the sale void. In the same year Michael Reese sued Gordon claiming the interest on his mortgage was not being paid. He started to foreclose on the property but Gordon claimed the Supreme Court decision had rendered the title worthless. Real estate title in the early days was indeed a most vexing problem!

Another of Gordon's law suits concerned land in Santa Clara County. In 1853, while visiting San Jose, he bought a piece of property known as the Narvaez Ranch at a sheriff's sale for $5,800.00. He had bid on it, he claimed, at the urging of Henry Clarkson, with whom he had driven to San Jose to inspect some nearby quicksilver mines. On returning to San Francisco, however, Gordon decided he had been led "into a trap" and refused to pay. The Sheriff, Joseph W. Johnson, then resold the property for $150, sued Gordon for the balance of $5,650, and won. In 1853 Gordon appealed, asking that the case be placed in the United States courts, as he was an alien, but the State Supreme Court refused to transfer the case. In January 1854, Gordon paid $6,578.50 to satisfy the claim.

This decision of the State Supreme Court, under Chief Justice Hugh C. Murray, aroused Gordon's anger. In 1855 Murray was a candidate for renomination by the Know-Nothing party. Opposition to him was strong in San Francisco. For example, on August 9, 1855, the *Herald* published a letter opposing him signed by such leading citizens as A. A. Ritchie and Thomas Larkin. Later another letter appeared asking that the nomination not be given to heavy gamblers and intemperate judges. This was signed by William T. Coleman, Frederick Macondray, Gordon's partner Edward T. Steen, and many others. It is of interest that Murray's later biographers, while admitting he drank heavily and gambled, claimed that his legal decisions were correct and that he was highly respected in his profession.

So strong was the opposition to Murray that a mass meeting was held calling for the election of a man of "temperance, moral and religious attitudes." The day after, the *Alta* published a long letter from Gordon in which he denied an accusation that he had tried to bribe Murray by offering him $500 to decide the Supreme Court case in his favor. Returning to the subject of the Santa Clara County Sheriff's sale, Gordon claimed that the only other bidder, Henry Laurencel, was an employee of Clarkson, the man who had led him into the trap by a "deliberate plot" which cost him $7,500. Gordon continued: "For six years Judge Murray and I have lived in California, during that time no one has seen me gamble one dollar, or has seen me drunk, or ever saw my foot on the threshold of a brothel."

The following day a note appeared in the *Herald* from Laurencel denying Gordon's charges. But it is of interest that historian Lawrence Bulmore referred to Laurencel as of "questionable scruples."

Clarkson who was a Know-Nothing candidate for the State Assembly, was defeated by a large vote, but

Murray was re-elected by a narrow margin. San Francisco, however, voted two to one against Murray.

Gordon was also sued by James Brownell regarding a lumber agreement in 1856; this case was still in the courts in 1863. No wonder Doyle in his memoir of Gordon wrote: "He was always engaged in litigation about something."

During the decade of the 1850s it was the custom of prominent citizens to sponsor benefits for popular actors and musicians or for some charity. These were special performances and the proceeds were bestowed on a particular person or charity. If a charity, the performers served gratuitously. Gordon's name is seldom found on the list of sponsors. However, in 1855 he was a sponsor for a concert for Stephen C. Massett, a fellow Englishman who, in 1849, had appeared in the first public concert in California, in the Portsmouth Square School. On November 11, 1855, the *Herald* published an announcement addressed to Massett stating that due to the "recent financial disaster . . . your friends" will sponsor a benefit. Joining Gordon in signing the announcement were such well known men as John Bigler, Neely Johnson, John T. Doyle, Milton Latham and Sam Brannan. Massett, in his autobiography, *Drifting About,* recalled this incident. His bank had closed and he was "rendered penniless." The concert at the Metropolitan Theatre was a great success and gave him an opportunity, after a long absence from the stage, to start on a concert tour.

The year 1855 had seen South Park well launched, but neither then nor later did it give its founder any great financial profits. The following year, 1856, Gordon established the business that was to lead to his affluence.

6

Industry, Politics and Land Problems

While 1855 had been a year of remarkable activity for George Gordon, he entered into the new year of 1856 with his energy not in the least diminished. He was making plans to build the first sugar refinery in California, one capable of supplying all the needs of the Pacific Coast.

The spirit of San Francisco of the 1850s is recalled in a statement in the City Directory of 1856: "destined yet to be the grand metropolis of the Pacific, rivaling perhaps in riches and renown the great ones of antiquity, the greater ones of modern times." The *Alta* hailed the establishment of a new basic resource for the ambitious city: "The establishment of one sugar refinery is another movement to cut off the importation of other than raw sugars, besides giving employment to many hands, manufacturing within ourselves one of the great staple articles of trade."

To obtain capital to develop this factory Gordon, accompanied by his wife and daughter, traveled to New York. Having accomplished his mission, he sailed for home by way of Chagres on April 5 on the *Illinois*. It must have been a miserable passage. In his pamphlet *Safety at Sea,* published in 1860, Gordon claimed there were 1,150 passengers on board, although the inspectors had certified the ship had accommodations for only 645. Because of this overcrowding, the food was insufficiently cooked, and the saloon which was the passengers' sitting room was "occupied by a constant succession of meals without intermission" and was "never free from the nauseating smell of meals and dirt." The second cabin passengers, he claimed, were so packed in that they were "left to scramble over one another in the fetid close air, like pigs."

From Chagres, Gordon and his family crossed the Isthmus by railroad to Panama City just in time to witness the tragic events that occurred there on April 15, 1856. He described them in a long article titled "Panama Massacre," which was published in the San Francisco *Chronicle*. The background of the situation was that the completion of the railroad had brought to Panama widespread unemployment and a severe business depression. Bitterness developed toward the constant stream of Americans traveling through.

Gordon's account related that a steerage passenger who was in the Panama City market place about 5:30 p.m. was "tolerably drunk." He refused to pay a native vendor for a melon he had eaten. This resulted in a fight and other natives joined in, finally raiding and gutting several saloons. After darkness fell, the mob, now drunk, attacked passengers in the steamship depot. Soldiers arrived, but, instead of dispersing the mob, fired at the Americans. Gordon claimed 15 to 25 Americans were killed during the night. On the next day, the 16th, the disturbance had subsided and the survivors boarded the *John L. Stephens* for San Francisco. The steamer arrived May 1, and Gordon's article in the *Chronicle* appeared the following day.

More articles appeared during the next few days, attacking the government in Washington for its "negligence, parsimony, and stupidity" in not punishing the natives of Panama. The *Chronicle* editorially urged

GEORGE GORDON'S SAN FRANCISCO SUGAR REFINERY

At Harrison and Eighth. Shown is David Hewes' Steam Paddy removing sand dunes to be dumped in the bay for fill. Hewes was a brother-in-law of Leland Stanford.

that the United States seize the Isthmus from the Pacific to the Caribbean or "let California have the liberty to teach the Sambos of Panama a lesson." The indignation was so intense that on May 6 a mass meeting was held to discuss a filibuster expedition to Panama. The eccentric political reformer, C. E. "Philosopher" Pickett, addressed the crowd. A Virginian by birth, he expressed on this occasion the views of a radical southerner, charging that "England was backing up these Sambo and Indian savages of Panama."

The San Francisco to which the Gordons returned was still recovering from the financial depression of the past two years. The city government was ineffective and suspected of being corrupt. Crime flourished and criminals went unpunished. Two weeks after the Gordons returned, a San Francisco supervisor, James P. Casey, fatally wounded James King of William, editor of the *Bulletin*. This resulted in the formation of the second Committee of Vigilance under the leadership of William T. Coleman.

The second Vigilance Committee was controversial in 1856, and it has remained controversial to the present day. However, in the spring of 1856 there was no question that the sympathy of the majority of the merchant class was with the aims of the Committee. This was demonstrated by the effective action taken against the San Francisco *Herald,* then one of the largest and most successful newspapers in the state.

The day King was shot the *Herald* questioned the formation of the Committee, stating: "We wish to be understood as most unqualifyingly condemning the movement." The city's powerful importers thereupon urged the main advertisers in the *Herald,* the auctioneers, "to advertise your sales in some other of the city papers." They did, and the *Herald* never regained its influence or the profits which it once commanded.

George Gordon showed considerable courage in disregarding the prevailing opinion of his class by questioning the benefits of the Vigilance Committee. He did so in a letter published in the *Chronicle* on July 26, 1856. He admitted that his opinion would prove unpopular and noted that "it is a source of regret to me that I am compelled to differ with many valued and intimate friends." He outlined his view that the Vigilance Committee had "violated the sacred compacts and guarantees of the Constitution of the United States for the sake of remedying local evils" and "subverted recognized law under the plea of administrating substantial justice." Then follows a long discussion of the "grandeur" of the American Constitution concluding that "the more the persons who attempt to violate it, the more excellent their characters, the more worthy their motives – the more dangerous is the example, the more serious is the crime." Curiously, the many studies that have been written about the 1856 Vigilance Committee have considered the views of other contemporaries, but Gordon's well balanced letter has not been cited.

The People's Party was formed as a result of the Vigilance Committee. Supported by the merchants and pledged to honesty and economy, it controlled the city's destiny for many years. On July 19, 1857, the *Alta* published the names of the candidates of the People's Party reform ticket. They were endorsed by most of the prominent businessmen of San Francisco, including George Gordon. This was unusual, as Gordon never became a citizen and customarily remained aloof from supporting any party or candidate. It appears he had made his peace with the powerful leaders of the reform movement, and he continued to endorse the People's Party candidates.

In spite of these turbulent events, Gordon continued in his efforts to establish his sugar refinery. The *California Chronicle* on July 19 noted that a group from "New York and San Francisco formed a company last winter" for its construction. The site Gordon selected was a large lot, 415 by 350 feet at the northwest corner of Harrison and Price (now Eighth) Street. It was, according to the San Francisco *Bulletin* of October 31, 1856, the former site of the Novelty Distillery Works, and machinery for the new factory had arrived on the clipper *Lotus*. The *Herald* had earlier described the plans for the sugar refinery: it would be of brick, and the Vulcan Foundry would erect the machinery. The sugar to be refined was expected to be obtained from "Manila and Batavia," according to the *California Chronicle*.

The next year the *Herald* added other possible sources of sugar cane: Siam, China, Formosa and Mexico. It is interesting that these distant sources are mentioned, while the nearer Hawaiian Islands, later to become a major source of cane, were still undeveloped.

The San Francisco Directory of 1856 described the completed refinery building as five stories high with a frontage of 75 feet and a depth of 122 feet. There were "two artesian wells which discharge 70,000 gallons of water per day." In its "General Review" of San Francisco events of the year, the Directory noted "ample supplies of cheap sugars of the East, and the extensive markets of the Pacific for the refined article" would "enable the company to command a large and profitable trade."

The office of the refinery was located with the firm of

Bond and Hale at 59 and 61 Sansome Street. C. W. Bond was one of the refinery's three trustees; the others were N. Chater and George Gordon. Henry M. Hale, who was later auditor of the City and County of San Francisco, became business manager and, according to one source, Gordon's confidential secretary.

On February 5, 1857, Alex Grogan wrote his business associate, Faxon Atherton, "The sugar refinery on Brannan [*sic,* actually Harrison] Street has commenced working and some sugar said to be of very superior quality is offered for sale. Little by little home production will supersede the imported articles and a portion of gold will remain here to be employed in railroads and other improvements." The San Francisco *Daily Town Talk* on February 25, 1857, also noted the refinery was in operation and described it.

One of the earliest and most detailed descriptions of Gordon's new venture appeared in April 1857 in *Hutchings' Illustrated California Magazine.* It stated that the article was "enabled" by the "polite attentions of George Gordon, Esq. the Principal." It noted that "this establishment belongs to an incorporated company, half of the stock in which is owned in San Francisco and half in the East." It gave a careful description of the method of producing sugar and of the buildings "located half way between San Francisco and the Mission." In addition to the main refinery, there was a brick engine house, a "bone-black factory," "a steam cooperage" and a "boarding house for hands" on the grounds. There were also facilities for making barrels. "A line of clipper barks are employed by the company," it continued, "to run between Batavia and Manila and this port for the purpose of importing sugar." An engraving of the factory illustrated the article.

Two lengthy articles expressing pride in Gordon's refinery appeared in the *Alta* in 1857. One, on November 21, stated the refinery would soon be producing enough barrels of refined sugar to supply not only California but also Oregon and Lower California, and since the distance from the sugar's source was less to San Francisco than to New York, the refinery would undersell the eastern United States. The second article described the refinery and the method of refining sugar, and praised both the refinery and "the enterprising spirit of the gentlemen who have engaged in so expensive an undertaking and who have achieved a flattering success."

Gordon's sugar won acclaim in 1857 at the State Agricultural Fair and at the Mechanics' Institute's annual exhibition of California products. The State Fair gave a framed certificate to the San Francisco Sugar Refinery, while the Mechanics' Institute judges commented that "productions of this manufactory cannot be excelled and the general admiration which they excited gives evidence that they are well entitled to a diploma."

There were both Irish and German workers at the refinery, and on April 26, 1858, the *Alta* reported a riot. Apparently there had been bad feelings between the two groups and the trouble started when an engineer named Hughes spoke of "Dutchmen." The refinery probably employed more Irish than Germans. Four years later, in 1862, Father Hugh Gallagher, pastor of St. Joseph's Church wrote to Archbishop Joseph Sadoc Alemany that ". . . of the 150 unmarried men working at the nearby sugar refinery, two-thirds of them heard mass."

In June 1858 the San Francisco Sugar Refinery increased its shares of capital stock and offered shares to the public, stating, "Although the profits of the company are not of that exaggerated character promised by undertakings, yet they will be found worthy of the attention of parties who desire to employ capital in an enterprise of a matured and successful character. . ." The next year, at a meeting of the stockholders on May 26, capital stock was again increased to $300,000.

The *State Register* of 1859 summed up the condition of the refinery at the end of the decade. It described the ownership as being "a company of San Francisco merchants" and stated that the "capacity is sufficient to supply the entire consumption of sugar in this state." It claimed that "a line of clipper barks is now employed in maintaining a regular supply."

Gordon's Vulcan Foundry had also been progressing. It announced in the 1856 City Directory that it was now the Vulcan Iron Works, still located "next to the Gas Works." In January 1855, according to the announcement, the foundry had been converted into an incorporated joint stock company, "the proprietors being Geo. Gordon, E. T. Steen, Paul Torquet, Sam'l Aiken and Charles R. Steiger." Torquet, Aiken and Steiger were former departmental heads at the foundry. Both Gordon and Steen withdrew from leadership of the firm in 1858. By then the company employed between "forty-five to ninety hands" and was doing an annual business of $170,000. George Gordon apparently remained connected to a certain extent with the Vulcan Iron Works, as he continued periodically to use its address in his advertisements. Joseph Moore, who became associated with the foundry in the 1850s, noted in his memoirs that Gordon was not a practical mechanic but a business man.

Gordon also continued active in public affairs. In August 1856, when the Sisters of Mercy were making efforts to establish "a Charity Hospital and Magdalen Asylum," Gordon became a member of the committee which, through notices in the newspapers, called upon the people of San Francisco to support this project. This institution became St. Mary's Hospital, the first Catholic hospital on the Pacific Coast.

Another civic affair to which George Gordon's name was linked was the celebration of the completion of the Atlantic telegraph cable in 1858. Gordon was a member of the committee sponsoring the parade and celebration held on September 27 to honor "American genius and American enterprise." The newspaper report of the completion of the Atlantic cable indicates an excitement analogous to that inspired by trips to the moon somewhat over a century later.

Gordon also gained fame as an orator. On January 3, 1858, the *Alta* announced that a Robert Burns Centennial would be held. George Gordon was elected president of the commemoration, and over his name notices appeared announcing a banquet to be held at the Oriental Hotel, tickets to cost ten dollars.

Gordon's speech at the banquet was so highly appreciated that several newspapers carried extensive sections of the text, and it was reprinted in full in a book published in 1870, and, in part, in another published in 1880. When one considers the fate of Gordon's own family, one passage becomes pertinent:

Is there no handwriting on the wall at this high festival? Shall we exalt in our poet's glory and take no warning? . . . He whom Scotland loved is smitten by Scotland's vice, and shall we not cry out? . . . Not with words of blame, but in accents of sorrow would we recall the spectacle of that spirit of beauty, degraded and dragged captive by animal appetite – of that glorious effluent of divinity obscured and polluted by the craving fiend of strong drink.

Gordon also made efforts to aid his friends, as established members of a community often do. In a letter written on March 6, 1858, to Russell Heath, assemblyman from Santa Barbara, he asked that Francisco Herrera, who served as consul for various Central and South American countries, be considered for the position of translator of laws. Gordon wrote that he had known Herrera for several years and considered him "a fine Spanish and English scholar, as consul for New Granada and as a Spanish teacher." He added that "Madame Herrera, an English lady, a teacher of high standing and many years experience, possesses a thorough knowledge of the idioms of the English and Spanish and could render him efficient aid." For a number of years Marie Herrera conducted the fashionable South Park Young Ladies Seminary, located on property once owned by Gordon at the northwest corner of Second and Bryant. The Atherton children attended the school in 1861.

There must have been few days during Gordon's years in California when he was not involved in some litigation. Difficulties over San Francisco land titles continued to plague him. One concerned the Santillan claim, which was based on a deed dated February 10, 1846, and consisted of 15,000 acres in the city. The claim was an alleged grant by Governor Pio Pico to Jose Prudencio Santillan, an Indian parish priest at Mission Dolores, of all vacant lands south of California Street. Bolton and Barron, members of a powerful pioneer San Francisco firm, later obtained this grant, and in June 1855 it was confirmed to them by the United States Land Commission.

Lands owned by George Gordon were of course involved. On February 3, 1859, the *Alta* reported a mass meeting held at "Musical Hall" to protest the "Santillan swindle." Gordon was a vice president of the committee. As a result of this meeting, a letter was sent to the Attorney General of the United States urging investigation of the land claim. In addition, a petition containing 8,136 names, of which Gordon had obtained 250, was sent to the Congress in Washington protesting the claim. Finally, the United States Supreme Court resolved the matter by rejecting the Santillan claim as a fraud.

Late that year, Gordon's property was jeopardized by the Sherreback claim to a vast section of San Francisco which included much of Rincon Hill and South Park. The United States District Court had just confirmed this title. Again a committee was formed to protest. Gordon, with Thomas Selby, A. J. Pope and a few others, filed a notice on December 10, 1859, asking those affected to contact the secretary of the committee, Henry Haight. A rehearing was held, and the claim was dismissed as invalid in 1860.

The Peter Smith titles also threatened Gordon's holdings. They had their origin in 1850 when Dr. Smith contracted with the city to care for the indigent sick in his hospital for $4.00 per patient per day. A year later, the city owed Dr. Smith $64,431.00. This claim was not disputed, but the city, lacking cash, paid him in scrip drawing 36 percent a year interest. The debt owed him soon became enormous. Smith sued and won, and a vast amount of city land was sold at a sheriffs' sale to speculators at low prices in order to pay Smith. The historian Theodore Hittell wrote that "the city was despoiled." During the Rodman Price trial in 1862,

Gordon related that he "owned five 100 vara lots held under Alcalde grants, accompanied by possession, which were adversely claimed by the holder of a Peter Smith title, in consequence of which I have repeatedly attempted but failed to sell, everything else being satisfactory to persons who wanted to purchase." The resolution of this vexation is not known.

Lastly, the famous Limantour claim affected Gordon's South Park property, a problem that was to harass Gordon's heirs after his death.

The decade of the 1850s in San Francisco ended with a tragic event – the most famous duel in California's history – the Broderick-Terry duel. It was an indirect outgrowth of the struggle between the North and the South. Through a series of complex events, United States Senator David C. Broderick, a northern sympathizer, was challenged by the Chief Justice of the Supreme Court of California, David S. Terry, a southerner. The duel took place on September 13, 1859. Terry shot Broderick, who died three days later.

Broderick in death was a martyr; newspapers which, while he was alive, had damned him as a corrupt politician, now acclaimed him as an heroic statesman. On September 24, a committee of leading citizens, including George Gordon, announced through the newspapers that a mass meeting would be held to raise funds for a suitable monument in his honor. The efforts of the committee were successful and the monument erected on Lone Mountain was described as "the most conspicuous in Laurel Hill Cemetery."

By 1860, Gordon had become a leader in San Francisco, and while he remained an alien, he had become a strong partisan of public causes in his adopted city and country.

7

Public Controversies

The Bulkhead question was one of the most controversial issues ever to confront San Francisco. It had its origin in 1856, when the contracts under which the wharves had been built were drawing to an end. The men who held the contracts had for many years controlled the entire waterfront and enjoyed huge profits. Reluctant to lose control of so valuable a property, they proposed building a stone bulkhead or sea wall along the waterfront. This improvement was needed, but they requested that they receive as compensation "the entire and exclusive right of wharfage, dockage, anchorage, and tolls within the city limits, with the sole right to regulate wharves, dockage and tolls" for fifty years. They organized the San Francisco Dock and Wharf Company to advance their proposal.

Its leader was Levi Parsons, a former district judge of San Francisco, whose term of office had been enlivened by a violent quarrel with the San Francisco press. Behind the project, however, was the powerful banking firm of Pioche, Bayerque and Company, which in turn was supported by French capitalists. François L. A. Pioche, who headed the firm, was one of San Francisco's most important financiers.

When the Bulkhead Scheme, as it came to be called, was first proposed in 1856, some of the city aldermen were favorably inclined toward it. Opposition developed gradually; it came especially from the newspapers and the mercantile community. In 1857 the Chamber of Commerce denounced the project, and in 1860 referred to it as the "machinations of a few foreign capitalists."

George Gordon was one of the first to attack the scheme. In 1856 he wrote a letter from his Vulcan Foundry office which was published on June 12 in the *California Chronicle*. In it he stated that although the waterfront was the most valuable asset of the city, yet the aldermen wanted to give it to a private company. He called the contract a "swindle" and "shockingly stupid." Then, referring to the aldermen favorable to the scheme, he became poetical, apparently paraphrasing a current jingle:

> For we're all jobbing,
> job, job, jobbing,
> For we're all jobbing
> about a Bulkhead.

Six days later, the same newspaper published on its front page another letter in which Gordon criticized the proposed contract paragraph by paragraph. He called it a "brief" on the covenant, the full text of which had been published in the *Alta* on June 9. Gordon described the scheme as "like a persimmon, nice to look at, but very astringent and unpleasant when it has to be masticated and swallowed." The *Chronicle's* editor, Frank Soulé called Gordon's letter "a masterly exposition of the attempted Bulkhead swindle."

The matter was still under investigation in 1859, when Gordon testified regarding the Bulkhead question before a special State Assembly committee. He explained he had "no pecuniary interest" and then gave his qualifications to testify, which included constructing the foundations of various buildings on the filled land of the waterfront in 1850 and 1851.

The Legislature did not vote on the measure until the next year, but as the time grew closer, excitement increased. On March 7, 1860, an executive committee was formed by the anti-Bulkhead groups to address a memorial to the Legislature. George Gordon was a member of this committee, which included Albert Dibblee, George Howard, Judge H. P. Coon, Lafayette Maynard, and William G. Babcock who a few years before had favored the scheme. On March 13, Gordon addressed a mass meeting at the Mechanics' Institute that was described as a Mechanics' anti-Bulkhead protest.

On March 21, the *Herald* printed a very long article of Gordon's entitled "The Extent, Cost and Revenue of the Bulkhead." (It was later published as a pamphlet titled "Parsons' Bulkhead.") In it he explained that even with a sea wall, deposits of mud would exist and dredging would be necessary. He objected to the cost of the project and offered a counter-proposal: he would build the wall himself in two, not six years as proposed by Parsons' San Francisco Dock and Wharf Company. Further, he would give the sea wall back to the public in ten or twenty years rather than fifty. And at no cost to the taxpayers.

Gordon further wrote of the "plundering nature" of the Bulkhead Scheme, "the shameless imprudence . . . the soft headed and wicked hearted credulity of its Legislature supporters" and the "infamy its unblushing jobbery brings upon the state."

This article was addressed to state senator Henry Edgerton, a leader of the Bulkheaders who represented Napa, Solano and Yolo counties. "We have doubted your integrity," Gordon wrote harshly, "We have questioned your intelligence," and "we will take pleasure in crucifying your reputation as a statesman, upon that mass of impudence, avarice and fraud – the Parsons' Bulkhead Bill."

Edgerton retaliated on April 3, when he delivered an oration in the Senate attacking Gordon's article: "It comes from that third-rate sophomorical, anti-bulkhead orator, that indefatigable, incessant pamphleteer and newspaper scribbler. . . Through a member of this body, he has addressed the country in a communication, which, for its insulting attack, its arrogant and florid impudence, its puerile and tinsel logic, its gross ignorance and misrepresentation of the subject of which he treats, is without a parallel in the history of the controversy. And who is this George Gordon? Why, sir, morally, he is an animated mass of putrefaction. His name is a proverb of infamy and contempt throughout the State. He first seeks to corrupt, and then libels our courts. An alien – he is the open, avowed enemy of our government, and a villifier of our institutions. A rejected, cast-off applicant for admission to the clubs of San Francisco, he sulks through the community, a despised, shunned, suspected, and guilty thing. ["Sensation," the legislative reporter noted.] Today, his fate trembles between ignominious flight from the country and incarceration in a prison. Why, sir, I hold in my hand a letter, accompanying the document which he addressed to myself through the columns of the San Francisco *Herald*. He refers me to certain gentlemen named therein, to find out who and what he is. I have given him the benefit of his reference. [Laughter and applause.] One of the gentlemen to whom he has referred, told me substantially, that he was the most consummate villain that ever went unhung. [Great laughter and applause.]"

Oscar T. Shuck in his 1901 *History of the Bench and Bar of California* referred to Edgerton's philippic against George Gordon as "perhaps the severest and most eloquent production of its kind ever spoken in our legislature."

The day following this philippic, the *Alta* described Edgerton as "a drunkard and addicted to another vice, which the law pronounces a felony and usually resulting with visits to the penitentiary." It continued:

> What is he today – He stands before the people – a disgraced and ruined man – doomed to eternal infamy and eternal punishment. He has turned like a viper upon those whose trusting generosity warmed him into life. He has betrayed his constituents and brought shame on his party. . .
>
> He has shown that from the first he was a slave to a corrupt and mercenary band of foreign monopolists and their tools. He has proved false to every principle which an honest man holds dear. And after passing through all the stages of trickery and fraud, he has closed his history by discharging the reeking contents of a filthy mind upon himself.

In those days journalism was often vehement and personal, and reprisals sometimes involved violence.

In spite of all the opposition, the bill passed the Assembly on April 13, and, as it had previously passed the Senate, was sent to Governer John Downey. When, on April 17, he vetoed the bill, the news was greeted with amazing enthusiasm, and the Governor became the hero of San Francisco. On May 1, 1860, the city celebrated the defeat of the scheme with a "Great Veto Jubilee." There was a torchlight procession, a "Gorgeous Pyrotechnic Display," a "Vast Concourse of People" and "Bonfires on the Heights," to quote some of the newspaper headlines. The parade started at the Wharf and made its way along Montgomery Street, across Market and to Second, to Howard, and then down Third Street to end at South Park. There, amidst "a perfect ovation," the governor "alighted from his barouche" and was escorted to the home of his private secretary, George Wallace, at 29 South Park.

The *Alta* reported later, "The celebration, exemplifying as it does, the enthusiastic willingness of our people to recognize and sustain official integrity and courage will long be remembered as a landmark in the history of California."

Gordon had contributed to the final event of the Bulkhead drama by donating $20 through the Sugar Refinery to "Gov. Downey's Reception."

The Bulkhead was not the only problem to which George Gordon directed his attention during 1860. One of his most remarkable pamphlets, *Safety at Sea,* appeared that year. Three years earlier, concerned with the safety of passengers at sea, he had written three articles containing some of the ideas expressed in this pamphlet. These were printed in the *Bulletin* under the signature, "An Englishman." The pamphlet appeared in November 1860. It was addressed "To the Honorables J. P. Benjamin, Wm. M. Gwin, E. D. Baker, J. W. Nesmith, senators of the United States, on the steamer *Sonora,* en route from San Francisco to New York," which left on November 11. Gordon explained that because of "the accident of four senators of the United States taking a long voyage together, during which they will have the enforced leisure of over three weeks," he was presenting them with his "observations on a subject of great importance."

In nineteen pages Gordon discussed four major causes of danger at sea: leaks, conflagration, the breaking of machinery, and overcrowding. To prevent leaks he suggested water-tight compartments which could be sealed off separately. To prevent fire he suggested that the engine rooms be equipped so flames could be put out with sea water. He also advised fire-resistant screens for the cabin lamps. In addition he presented ideas for improved ventilation, suggesting that fresh air be furnished to the engine rooms and steerage quarters. He attacked the customary over-crowding on the vessels claiming the passengers were "cribbed, cabined and confined" and suffered from poor food, lack of water, and lack of space.

To implement the needed reforms, Gordon recommended a commission with power to prosecute the ship owners who violated the safety standards. In many of his suggestions Gordon was years ahead of his time. The *Alta* on November 11 praised his suggestions, stating "The pamphlet is a masterly one and does no less credit to Mr. Gordon's business talent than his public spirit and his forcible pen."

Twenty months later, on July 27, 1862, a great disaster occurred when the steamer *Golden Gate* burned off Manzanillo, Mexico, while south-bound from San Francisco to Panama. More than two hundred lives were lost. Gordon wrote a lengthy letter about the disaster, which appeared on the front page of the *Alta* of August 11, 1862. Repeating some of the warnings in his 1860 pamphlet, he also charged that "seven hundred were jeopardized by the folly and meanness of one man." Here Gordon was referring to Commodore Vanderbilt on whose ship *Northern Light* Gordon himself and his family had been passengers a few months before. "True we were not burnt or drowned," Gordon added, referring to that voyage, "despite the recklessness of the owner of the *Northern Light*."

In 1860 Gordon had charged Senator William M.

Gwin with "legislating for the benefit of the Pacific Mail Company." This was not a new charge. For example, the *Bulletin* on November 27, 1856, had published a letter which stated "It is generally believed that Gwin is a special agent of the Pacific Mail Steamship Company."

Gordon's letter, written in New York on May 8, 1860, was titled "Memorial of Californians in New York" and was signed by Theodore Payne and Peter Donahue, as well as its writer. Brought to San Francisco by Pony Express, it was published in the *Bulletin* on May 23. (It had also appeared in the *New York Times* on May 8, 1860.) It voiced support of Senator John P. Hale's Overland Mail bill. A mail route overland would, of course, be a blow to the Pacific Mail Steamship Company. The letter expressed the opinion that if the California representatives in Congress supported this bill it would pass. Gordon also maintained that the people were weary of the "babbling north and an angry south." He was referring to the bitter battles in Congress regarding whether the transcontinental stage and railroad routes should cross the continent in the south or the north. Hale had suggested a compromise in his bill.

Gwin replied to Gordon's allegations in a letter published in the *Bulletin* on June 9. He maintained Gordon had been led into error "by designing men, the most adroit of whom is I. C. Woods, well known in California as president of the Adams and Company Express." He referred to the Adams and Company failure and Wood's subsequent flight.

Hale's bill did not pass, and the *Alta,* a newspaper always quite critical of Gwin, on July 24, 1860, declared Gwin was a factor in the defeat. Gwin's enemies claimed his expenses for sumptuous entertaining were footed by the Pacific Mail, "loath to lose their monopoly of transportation to and from the West." Lately Thomas, in his biography of Gwin, answers these charges by claiming Gwin was "the whipping boy for every sin committed by the Chivalry."

Still another important topic of that period, the validity of titles to mining rights, was of active interest to Gordon. On October 28, 1859, the Montgomery Street bookseller, John G. Gilchrist, published a pamphlet printed by Towne and Bacon, entitled *Mining Titles – Are There Any – What Are They? A letter to the Vice President of the Quartz Mining Association.* It was signed by Gordon, who referred to himself as a "fellow miner." He said that in 1857 and 1858 he had been interested in a "promising mine in Southern California," and had obtained not only $100,000 in capital from Scotland but found ten or twelve Scotch families willing to emigrate to work the mine. His project, he continued, was injured by a recent court decision relating to the New Almaden mine (United States vs. Parrott) in which the court denied the public the right to mine on public land. Gordon contended that the government was not the owner of mineral rights on public land, that the mines belonged to the people and should be free to any worker. The New Almaden mercury mine, named after the centuries-old Almaden mine of Spain, was discovered before the Gold Rush. It became of vast importance, as quicksilver was needed by the gold mines to separate the gold from its ore. In 1850 the firm of Barron and Forbes, which included John Parrott, controlled the mine. It is well said that the mine was "famous for its wealth and notorious for its long tempestuous life in the courts."

In 1858 the courts upheld a claim that halted operations at the mine briefly the next year. The claim was owned by Henry Laurencel, who had aroused Gordon's enmity a few years before in connection with his Sheriff's-sale purchase of land in Santa Clara county. This involvement of Laurencel may have been a factor in the position Gordon assumed.

A San Francisco newspaper of 1860 aptly summed up the outward signs of George Gordon's public concerns when it noted, "Mr. George Gordon seems to have a mania for letter writing."

8

The Early 'Sixties

George Gordon had visited New York in 1860 in the interest of the Sugar Refinery. Accompanied by his family, as in 1856, he sailed from San Francisco on April 27 on the *Northern Light*. The month before, he had received a letter from William T. Coleman, then living in New York, indicating that they could do "considerable together . . . to our mutual advantage." Coleman proposed to Gordon that his merchandising house would buy the raw sugar for the firm and sell the refined, "thus giving you your full time, energies [and] means to the working of your Refinery." Although Gordon apparently discussed the matter with Coleman in New York, he did not accept the suggestion at that time, as will be mentioned later.

Gordon also attended to other affairs in New York, including the sale of some property he owned at 538 Hudson Street. It was reported that he also went to Europe to buy machinery for the expanding sugar refinery, but if so it was a brief trip, for he was away from San Francisco only four months in all.

The early 'sixties were years of affluence for Gordon, as indicated by receipted bills in the author's possession and elsewhere. He and his family were living in a style befitting residents of the elite park he had created. His purchases while in the East included frock and dress coats, jewelry from Shreve and Brown of Boston, and monogrammed goblets, champagne glasses, wine glasses and finger bowls from the Boston and Sandwich Glass

Company. After returning to San Francisco on September 2 aboard the *John L. Stephens,* he continued spending money quite freely. The bills from George Poultney's South Park Livery Stable show he hired three carriages to call for him and his entourage when the ship docked. He also rented carriages for the theater and a rockaway for Sunday drives. He purchased saddles from Main and Winchester and books from Josiah Lecount. He had his South Park residence painted and repaired and bought for it furniture, curtains, carpets, and window drapes.

Mrs. Gordon, in the meantime, was buying large quantities of fashionable clothing from such stores as the City of Paris; its bills stated: "Payable in U.S. gold coin." From at least 1859 on, Gordon rented a pew at Trinity Church, paying ten dollars a month, not an insignificant sum a hundred years ago. Nor were his bills for liquors that year small, a fact that may be considered significant considering the later history of the family. For example, on September 21 he paid V. Marziou $23.00 for six cases of claret, on November 9 he paid Fox and Melville $205.30 for unspecified wines and ales, and in December he purchased from Van der Meden a gallon of brandy for $9.00 and a gallon of sherry for $6.00. (See illustration at page 188.)

San Francisco's business, civic and political activities also continued to occupy Gordon's attention. He became a life member of the Young Men's Christian Association in 1860, seven years after its founding in San Francisco. On April 10, 1861, he received recognition from the powerful business world when he was elected to the Chamber of Commerce and shortly after was appointed to the committee on appeals. That same month he joined other leaders, including John Parrott and William C. Ralston, in addressing a letter to United States Senator Milton S. Latham advising him of their "cordial approval" and of their desire to have a public dinner in his honor on his return to California from Washington.

George Gordon was an active member of the St. Andrews Society, which as early as 1850 was taking part in parades, such as those celebrating Washington's Birthday, and conducting festivals. However, it was not formally organized until 1863. On November 7 of that year Gordon became its 172nd member, and at its first banquet gave a toast entitled "The Land of Cakes," referring to Scotland's famed oatmeal cakes. The *Alta* reported that Gordon had lauded "the sons of Scotland: distinguished in the past and present days in various professions and vocations of life." At the November 30, 1864, banquet Gordon spoke on the "Growing Commerce of San Francisco." The minutes of the St. Andrews Society, which escaped destruction in 1906, disclose that Gordon took an active part in the organization and often gave financial aid.

During the early days of San Francisco, the Fire Department was composed of volunteer companies, organizations of both social and political power. In May 1863 a ball was given in the newly opened Union Hall on Howard Street by the Liberty Hose Company No. 2, located at 147 Fourth Street. Gordon was a member of the committee, and again on November 19 he was a member of the committee sponsoring the first "Grand Ball" of all the city's fire companies, also held in Union Hall.

Local San Francisco events of the first half of the decade of the 1860s were, however, overshadowed by the catastrophic Civil War, and Gordon characteristically articulated his views on the conflict. In 1861, on the eve of the war, he wrote an article which appeared in the *Bulletin* and was later printed by Towne and Bacon as a twenty-one page pamphlet. The article was entitled "The National Crisis, A letter to the Hon. Milton S. Latham, Senator from California in Washington." Gordon discussed from his vantage point as an Englishman the many differences between the North and South. "Though not technically a citizen [of the United States] all my interests are bound up in the welfare and progress of its people," he wrote. He believed there was freedom in the North but not in the South, where labor was not held in honor. "If the South was to abolish slavery tomorrow – were the negroes free – the ethnological repulsion, the unconquerable antipathy of race would prevent the negro's admittance to equality with the white man in political power and privilege." He wrote of the divisions in America and expressed his opinion that the "middle class of Great Britain and New England has more affinity than a New Englander and a Carolinian." In California, where there was no slavery, he continued, "the Northerners work, developing the resources of the country in mining, farming, etc., while the Southerners become our legislators, statesmen, lawyers, and government officials." Referring to the Southern tradition of defending honor by dueling, he stated, "Broderick the Roundhead lost his life by submitting in a moment of weakness to a cavalier's ordeal – that of skill with a pistol." He predicted that the South would never submit, for "aristocracy never did submit willingly." While he also predicted that California would remain in the Union and that no Pacific Republic would develop, he questioned that "freedom should be baptized in blood" and urged calmness. Gordon's view was that union was not always strength, and that peaceful separation of the North and South might be advisable.

As the war proceeded, many conflicts between North and South sympathizers occurred in San Francisco. On September 28, 1864, Gordon was attacked by the provocative, often rabble-rousing newspaper, *The American Flag*. It claimed that one George Pearce "a poor laboring man, having a large family dependent on his labor was discharged . . . from the Sugar Refinery . . . for no other offense than being loyal to the land of his birth." The attack continued, "This Sugar Refinery . . . is owned by an English alien, George Gordon. This scandalous case of political persecution [is] being brought to the notice of Deputy Collector Phillips. It is sufficient to stamp the name of the perpetrators with eternal infamy."

Gordon answered at once, replying in the October 1 *News Letter* that he "never asks or knows concerning their [the employees] political preferences," and that only once had he interfered, and that was when Leland Stanford, a Republican, and John McConnell, a Democrat, were contesting for the governorship. Then he had "interposed to inform the men that he deemed the election of a man of Southern and Secession proclivities [a] dangerous step." Gordon also said that there was no George Pearce who had ever been employed at the Refinery, but that there had been one George Pearson, "described as single and Irish." This man had been employed to replace a regular hand who was sick. When the regular hand had returned, Pearson was discharged. Also Gordon explained that after each payday, Pearson was absent. Lastly Gordon addressed his remarks to the editors of *The American Flag,* stating,

"Vituperation and falsehood are doubtless efficient weapons in a political campaign, when agents sufficiently devoid of honor can be engaged to use them [but] men of ordinary calibre will find a decent respect for truth most useful to them."

On April 15, 1865, less than a week after the surrender at Appomattox, San Francisco learned of President Abraham Lincoln's tragic assassination. George Gordon was among those who signed a notice, published in the *Alta,* of a meeting of British citizens at the British Consulate concerning the "deplorable calamity" and asking permission to join in the "obsequies of the late lamented President."

Four days later there was a great procession honoring the slain leader. The English resident contingent and the St. Andrews Society members were among the fifteen thousand men who marched in the solemn procession. It crossed Market from Montgomery Street, proceeded up Second to Folsom, then turned west on its way to the Mechanics' Institute building in Union Square. On the steep hill on Second Street above Folsom stood the elite of Rincon Hill and South Park, still at that time the city's most fashionable district. Photographs show the beautifully dressed ladies and the men in their frock coats and top hats.

An aftermath of this event was the organization of the British Benevolent Society, with membership offered to "all persons born under the British Flag." George Gordon became an active member.

The Gordon family appeared to be occupying an established position in the social life of the city. An example of the acceptance of the Gordons is their presence at Mrs. William E. Barron's ball in 1863. It was an enthusiastically heralded event. As one newspaper noted, "For a fortnight past the fashionable world of San Francisco has been agitated by a single subject, nothing else has been thought of, or talked about, or dreamed of but the approaching ball!"

It was given at the Barron's Stockton Street mansion in honor of Francesca Walkinshaw and Sam Price, who had recently been married at the Hacienda at New Almaden. One newspaper noted in its descriptions of the guests, "Mrs. Gordon was also arrayed in excellent taste in a dress of magenta silk with flounces of black lace which by a certain style bespoke its Parisian origin," and "Pretty little Miss Gordon looked like a fair Proserpine gathering flowers, herself a fairest flower, looped up with a cordon of straw and a bouquet of field flowers."

In the summer of 1861 Gordon and his family were guests at the Geyser Springs. It was the custom in the latter part of the last century for San Franciscans of means who did not own country estates to spend part of the summer at fashionable resorts. The *Alta* of June 27 noted the arrival of the Gordons at the Geysers. On the same day "Mr. and Mrs. Doyle of San Francisco" arrived. John T. Doyle was in New York on that date, but his parents or his brother Emmett may have traveled with the Gordons.

In 1861 the Geysers, with its great steam jets, was an attraction no visitor to California cared to miss, and the resort was advertising itself as the "wonder of the world." Dr. Winslow Anderson was to later describe it as a "branch of Hades nestling among the umbrageous oaks and firs in pine clad mountains surrounded on all sides by his Satanic Majesty's prodigious laboratory." This resort, where the author spent several weeks in 1917, has now had its steam harnessed by the Pacific

Gas and Electric Company for generating electric power.

The federal tax records for 1863 show George Gordon as owning two one-horse carriages and one two-horse carriage. The latter had been noted in the *Alta* the year before. On September 20, 1862, the *Alta,* on its front page, had informed its readers of "A narrow Escape." When Mrs. Gordon's carriage was descending Rincon Hill by the steep, unpaved slope of Second Street to Folsom "one of the neck yoke straps broke and the horses, a span of sorrels, became unmanageable and started down the hill." The coachman rescued Mrs. Gordon, who escaped serious injury.

One of the most notable law suits in which Gordon became involved concerned Rodman McCamly Price. Price had been a leading man of affairs, a prominent member of San Francisco's early business community. Returning to the East in 1851, he became first a congressman and then governor of New Jersey. While in San Francisco, prior to his departure, Price acquired a great deal of real estate; in fact, Price claimed he owned "more houses in 1850-1851 than any other person." However, in 1853, his property was heavily mortgaged. On leaving California he gave his power to deal with his interests to Edmund Scott, and later, when Scott was visiting in South America, to General Erasmus Keyes. When Scott returned, Price gave power of attorney to Keyes and Scott jointly.

In 1853 Keyes and Scott sold Price's property for $135,000 to Theodore Payne and Squire Dewey. Shortly afterwards property values rose greatly and the new owners realized a profit of several hundred thousand dollars. Price, angered, filed suit against Payne, Dewey, Scott and Keyes for $500,000, alleging fraud. Aiding

Price in his defense was the powerful Sam Ward, who had been in California during the Gold Rush and who was known in Washington as "King of the Lobby."

John T. Doyle, then living in New York, became Dewey's attorney and defended him successfully. On behalf of the defendants, depositions were taken from prominent San Francisco landowners. These included Hall McAllister, Horace P. Janes, Horace Hawes, A. J. Bowie, Michael Reese, James Lick, Colonel E. D. Baker and George Gordon.

This case came before the New York Supreme Court in 1862. The printed testimony fills five bound volumes and contains a great deal of information regarding San Francisco property in the Gold Rush period.

Gordon's deposition, taken December 27, 1860, was twenty-three pages long. In it he defended Dewey and Payne, testifying that the sum for which they bought Price's property was fair for the time. He told how during the past ten years he had bought and sold real estate in San Francisco "to the amount of about half a million dollars" and knew land values. Like others who testified, he explained how in 1850 and 1851 property values were extremely high; they fell substantially between January 1852 and January 1853, then rose once more in July 1853, and slowly receded in 1854. Depression, he stated, occurred with the failure of banking houses in 1855. Low prices then prevailed until the end of 1858.

Gordon enumerated the reasons the price of land was low when Keyes and Scott sold Price's real estate. These included the difficulties with squatters, the question of Alcalde titles, the cloud placed on property by the Limantour and Sherreback claims, and the Peter Smith titles.

Price did not win his case. However, the last case in the matter did not reach the courts until 1880. It was dismissed, the judge citing the fact that twenty-four years had elapsed since some of the contested events had taken place.

General Keyes, in his book *Fifty Years Observations of Men and Events* published in 1884, was still disturbed about this costly struggle. He was of the opinion that a jury in New York in 1860 could not understand the gold-rush days in San Francisco. He wrote that it was like having "a man who is charged with stealing a lump of ice in Alaska in January" tried in July by a judge and jury "who had never left Yuma."

On August 5, 1861, during the Civil War, Congress enacted an income tax. Gordon's large payments, $1,000 in 1862 and $1,361 in 1864, indicate his successful financial condition. This success led Gordon to follow the trend of the elite and create for himself an elaborate country estate.

9

Mayfield Grange

In 1863 Gordon established the estate on the Peninsula that was to be his home the remainder of his life. Its location in Santa Clara County was convenient because the railroad line from the city, still under construction, had been completed that far. The San Francisco and San Jose Railroad was one of the earliest railroad projects in California. Several attempts to construct it in the 1850s failed. Finally, however, a group organized under the leadership of Peter Donahue, aided by such well known men as Henry M. Newhall, started work in 1861. By 1863 the railroad had crossed the southern San Mateo county line and was proceeding southward in Santa Clara County. To quote San Mateo County historian Frank M. Stanger: "The building of the railroad was followed almost immediately by a succession of men with famous names moving to establish homes down the Peninsula. . . Theirs were the first steps in the establishment of many elaborate county residences which the railroad would bring within easy reach of offices and social engagements in the city."

The land Gordon selected for his estate was just south of San Francisquito Creek, which divides Santa Clara and San Mateo counties, and west of the railroad which still today crosses the creek at the historic tall redwood tree, the "Palo Alto." North of Gordon's property, at what was called Fair Oaks, were the large estates of Faxon Atherton and Thomas Selby, while at nearby

Menlo Park were the residences of his friends William E. Barron and John T. Doyle.

Other neighbors during Gordon's presence at Mayfield Grange included John T. Doyle's brother, R. E. Doyle, his brother-in-law United States Senator Eugene Casserly, Myles Sweeney of the Hibernia Bank, and two wealthy former neighbors of Gordon's on Rincon Hill, Henry Dexter and George C. Johnson.

Gordon testified in an 1865 land case, United States vs. C. N. Rodriguez, that he became part owner in 1861 of the Rancho San Francisquito, "Little St. Francis." This ranch of 1,471 acres was granted in 1839 by Governor Alvarado to Antonio Buelna, whose widow was later married to Francisco Rodriguez.

In the early 1850s the ranch was divided into numerous small acreages, and among the newcomers settling there were William Little, Thomas Bevins and Thomas Wilson. Gordon obtained Wilson's and Little's lands as well as Bevins' farm. By 1865 he had acquired 572 acres.

Two adjoining ranchos had somewhat similar Spanish names. To the south, now part of Stanford University, was the Rancho Rincon de San Francisquito. To the east was Rancho Rinconada del Arroyo de San Francisquito, on which the city of Palo Alto is now located.

George Gordon approached this new project with characteristic enthusiasm. When visiting his property, he often called at the Doyle estate. "Mr. Gordon goes down every week to inspect his farm and to select a handsome location for his house," wrote John T. Doyle's mother in a letter to him dated January 20, 1863, and Doyle's sister later added a postscript: "Mr. Gordon has completed the purchase of the place across the creek and is about commencing to build." Doyle's

GORDON'S MAYFIELD GRANGE HOME AT PALO ALTO

Shown after being purchased by Leland Stanford, and somewhat enlarged by him.
It was further enlarged in the 1880s, and was demolished in 1965.

Courtesy of Clyde Arbuckle of San Jose.

JOHN T. DOYLE
Gordon's attorney and business associate.
Courtesy of Society of California Pioneers.

WILLIAM T. COLEMAN
"LION OF THE VIGILANTES"
Business associate of Gordon, and later
a contender with Gordon regarding owner-
ship of stock in the Sugar Refinery.
Courtesy of the California Historical Society.

THE DOYLE HOME AT MENLO PARK NEAR THE GORDON ESTATE
Photo by Muybridge; courtesy of the Bancroft Library.

Mr Geo Gordon

Bought of **FOX & MELVILLE,**

(Successors to FOX & O'CONNOR,)

Importers and Wholesale Dealers in

WINES, BRANDIES, ETC.

Corner of Clay and Leidesdorff Streets.

186o

March 18	1 C⁄	Albert	8	2	16	✓
	½ dz	Port	15	7 50	✓
April 2	2 Doz	Champagne	17	34 —	✓
	3 q	Claret	8	24 —	✓
	1 "	Sauterne		6 —	✓
Oct 11	2 dz	Claret	4	8 —	✓
Nov 1	1 Hhd	do		75 —	✓
		paid for bottles		28 06	
		" man for bottling		4	
				205.30	

1860 Nov 9th

Rec'd payment Fox & Melville

A Bill for Supplies for the Gordon Cellar

From the author's collection.

mother also reported, "Miss Nelly [*sic*] has finished her education at Christmas."

The estates and their owners clearly carried prestige, for when in 1863 Leander Ransome advertised his Menlo Park subdivision in the *Alta,* he mentioned its location as near the George Gordon, F. D. Atherton, Thomas Selby and George Johnson estates. In the following year in the same newspaper, John Middleton advertised land "adjoining the residences of George Gordon, F. D. Atherton and George Johnson."

Roy P. Ballard, writing in *The First Year at Stanford,* claimed Gordon was a 'fine business man and certainly good-hearted and generous, but he was no farmer." Nevertheless, according to an obituary in the *News Letter,* probably written by its editor Frederick Marriott, Gordon was credited with "bringing water for complete irrigation [and] planting an extensive vineyard with foreign grapes of his own selection from which he expected to make a superior quality of wine." In addition: "His active mind turned to the subject of the manufacture of beet sugar. He planted a large space of ground with beets, and endeavored to urge upon the farmers to do likewise."

Ballard's account continued: "He laid out several fine drives, including Eucalyptus Avenue, and built a very respectable house and stables. . . He was his own architect and when the carpenters were laying the second floor of the house, he remarked that he thought the ceiling would be too low, but he would see when it was finished. That evening returning from San Francisco, he decided it did not suit him and had it all taken out and changed regardless of cost."

Gordon named his estate "Mayfield Grange." The "Mayfield" was acquired from the nearby "Mayfield

Farm" established in 1853 by Elisha O. Crosby, who was serving as Lincoln's minister to Guatemala when Gordon was creating his estate. "Grange" recalled the nineteenth century English meaning of the word, a farm with a house, barns, etc., for a gentleman farmer. And Gordon became the English gentleman farmer. His house parties given there were "in the English manner, serving cold joints for breakfast, to the astonishment of some of the local gentry," according to the recollection of Amelia Ransome Neville in her book about San Francisco society, *Fantastic City*.

By 1864 Mayfield Grange had become the permanent home of the Gordons. The San Francisco address of 25 South Park was last listed in the City Directory of 1863-1864.

Mayfield Grange is now part of Stanford University, and in the University library is a map of the estate as surveyed by the civil engineer Alfred Poett. The map shows the location of not only the mansion but the outbuildings as well, all just south of San Francisquito Creek and west of El Camino Real. The outbuildings included a chicken house, stables and carriage house, which were situated in the orchards and gardens. In front of the house was a fountain. The Gordon home was a splendid dwelling described as "surrounded by broad balconies" from which "could be seen the loveliest view in the whole country."

In 1876, this beautiful estate was sold by Gordon's heirs to Governor Leland Stanford. He paid $170,000 for the property, according to the *San Francisco Real Estate Circular,* and renamed it "Palo Alto," the Spanish name for the great redwood tree that was the area's most prominent landmark. Stanford remodeled the house and enlarged it. He also increased the size of the estate until it contained over 7,200 acres. A document at the Stanford University Library indicates that Stanford purchased 650 acres from the Gordon heirs. However, according to the 1876 Thompson and West *Atlas of Santa Clara County,* the property appears to be larger. The probate records of Mrs. Gordon's estate, and later those of her brother, John James Clark, give the acreage for the property as 698 and 697 acres. Since Clark's widow sold the land shortly after her husband's death, 697 acres may be the correct size of the estate sold to Stanford.

After Governor and Mrs. Stanford's only child, Leland Junior, died in Florence, Italy, in 1884, the idea of founding a university to bear his name developed. Construction of the University began in 1885 on land south of the Stanfords' residential area, and the institution opened in 1891. In the earthquake of 1906, the Stanfords' house was badly damaged, especially an 1888 brick addition. It was repaired and later served for many years as the Stanford Children's Convalescent Hospital. Finally antiquated, it was demolished in 1965. The old timber became part of the annual Big-Game bonfire before the California-Stanford football game. What remained of Gordon's mansion, after a hundred years of occupancy, went up in smoke.

10

The Entry and Exit
of William T. Coleman

Nothing had come of Gordon's discussion in New York in 1860 about the possibility of William T. Coleman's firm serving as agent for the San Francisco Sugar Refinery. Gordon later claimed the negotiations had terminated because Coleman demanded sixty percent of the refinery's stock.

Gordon was planning an expansion of his sugar operations and was purchasing new equipment in spite of the fact that 1859 had not been a good year financially for his enterprise. The company owed George Gibbs $6,144, Parrott and Company $6,000, and Barron and Company (through Thomas Bell) $24,000. Gordon had pledged his South Park property as security on the note to Barron and Company.

At the beginning of 1860, the stock was distributed as follows: Gordon, 375 shares; his brother-in-law, John James Clark of England, 125 shares; P. W. Hale, 490 shares; James B. Bond, nine shares; and Henry Hale, one share. Gordon held the power of attorney for Clark's shares.

In February 1860, Hale and Bond sold their stock to Gordon for $62,000. Gordon later explained that at the close of 1859 cash was needed for the refinery's operations and that while he was willing to advance more funds, Hale was unable to do so. In 1860, Gordon also assumed the Chater claim against the refinery, which was fought in the courts for a number of years. Nathaniel Chater was one of the original trustees of the refinery. Gordon held that Chater, who was to have been manager, was "smitten with paralysis." Gordon himself then assumed Chater's duties, and he stated that as a result he had to sell his foundry in order to devote his entire time to the refinery. Gordon also held that Chater never placed any money in the firm and had misled those who did finance it by claiming it would cost only $37,000 to build. Actually, before the factory was finished, it had cost between $125,000 and $130,000.

At the first meeting of the company's officers on September 15, 1856, Chater was "voted out" as manager. James B. Bond was elected president and Gordon secretary. On December 2, 1856, another meeting was held and Hale was elected trustee in place of Chater, to serve with Bond and Gordon. At that time Gordon owned 375 shares, Hale 125 and Chater none. The Chater heirs alleged fraud, but eventually they lost their case.

After Bond and Hale withdrew as trustees of the refinery, they were replaced by Dr. William A. Douglass and Charles De Ro. Douglass, Gordon's personal physician and a witness of his will in 1865, was a longtime member of the San Francisco Board of Health. De Ro had long been associated with the refinery, and in 1860 had served as manager when Gordon was in the East. He was a resident of South Park and his daughter Charlotte was a friend of Nellie Gordon. In addition, De Ro was selling the refinery's sugar on his own account. He advertised in the *Alta* on September 17, 1860, that he had 200 pounds of sugar for auction from the San Francisco Sugar Refinery.

During this period of change in the refinery, the first bookkeeper, B. B. Gore, whom Gordon did not care for, was replaced by James Kellogg, who became secretary of the firm as well.

In July 1860 Gordon placed notices in the *Alta* offering shares of stock in the San Francisco Sugar Refinery and in the soon-to-be-built Pacific Sugar Refinery. One half of the shares in both refineries were to be sold; the current owners would retain the balance. Both refineries were dealing directly with planters in Manila, Java, Siam, Formosa and China, according to the notices. Shares could be obtained from Gordon, John Middleton and Son, or Nathan V. Maston, a real estate dealer who was also a neighbor of Gordon's in South Park.

Stock continued to be advertised for sale in 1861. Gordon explained in a notice of July 30 in the *Evening Bulletin* that while his refinery was eighth in size in the United States, there was need for enlargement to meet the increased demand for refined sugar on the Pacific Coast. By then the new refinery was under construction.

Although the *Alta* on February 20, 1861, had described it as being built and the *Mining and Scientific Press* carried another description a month later with a picture of it, construction was actually still underway at the end of 1862. The *Alta* on December 17 reported that the main building would be seven stories, while a two-story warehouse would be next to it.

A building for the production of bone charcoal was also being built. Water was to be supplied by the company's own wells, which gave 80,000 gallons per day, supplemented by the Spring Valley Water Company which would deliver an additional 10,000 gallons per day. The *Alta* stated that 130 men were employed at the old refinery and 115 more would be working in the new one.

Stock was still being offered for sale in 1863. In April, Gordon announced that the combined output of the two refineries would be the "largest or at least equal to the largest output of any refinery in the United States," and he informed the members of the "mercantile community who desire to become interested" that the stock could be obtained at "reasonable terms."

Meanwhile, in the spring of 1862, William T. Coleman's suggestion that he import the raw sugar for the company and sell the refined product had finally been accepted. This arrangement continued until the spring of 1863 when Coleman entered the firm as owner of one half of the shares. Since three trustees were needed, 150 shares were transferred to Thomas Bell, as agent for Barron and Company, with the understanding, according to Gordon, that he, Gordon, would control them. Gordon continued as manager of both refineries.

The certificate of incorporation of the San Francisco and Pacific Sugar Company, which finally combined the two companies and raised the capital stock to $800,000, was dated May 26, 1863. The number of trustees was increased to five. In addition to Gordon, Coleman and Bell, there were William Hooper, Henry Carlton, Jr. and H. B. William, the latter two San Francisco associates of William T. Coleman.

By the next spring, however, the close association between Gordon and Coleman was fast deteriorating. For instance, Coleman's lawyer apparently offended Gordon, for on May 12 Gordon wrote Coleman, "Whoever the legal luminary may be who emitted so brilliant a production, he has at least one mark of good sense, he withholds his name, which somewhat saves his reputation." He charged "your legal friend" with having "a confusion not uncommon to the bar" and rejected a statement made by the attorney with, "Ye Gods, what twaddle! I wonder when lawyers will think."

The relationship with Coleman continued to be uneasy. On May 20, 1864, Coleman wrote Gordon refusing to advance money, claiming the sugar market was dull. On July 1, he wrote Gordon, referring to Carlton's resignation as a trustee, and stated he had transferred Carlton's stock to Hooper. Coleman suggested that George Platt, his bookkeeper in San Francisco, replace Carlton as trustee. Gordon objected strenuously and suggested Rudolph Feuerstein, a local merchant and partner with Frederick Roeding in a hide and wool business.

It was in this same month, July, that Gordon discovered to his dismay that Coleman had obtained Bell's 150 shares, thus securing a majority of the shares of the company. Gordon wrote Coleman on July 5 protesting the action, accusing him of wanting "to control my property." He added, apparently consigning past disagreements to unimportance, "I regret that a pleasant and profitable intercourse of over two years with your company without a word of difference should have met with such an untoward interruption." He suggested that the stock be sold so that each would have an equal 3,850 shares. Gordon also called to Coleman's attention that the removal of the Barron interests "damaged the whole stock for sale." He had asked Bell to return the money to Coleman that he had received from the sale of the stock, but Bell refused to do so.

The difficulty continued, with Gordon offering suggestions and Coleman refusing them. In April 1865 Gordon urged Coleman to sell his stock to John Parrott, Nicholas Luning and Joseph Donohoe. Coleman replied that his stock was worth $250,000, but he would sell for $225,000 in cash or "paper" from either Parrott, Luning, Donohoe, Barron, George Howard or Faxon Atherton. For some reason, this plan did not mature. On June 23, Gordon sent Coleman $7,500 in gold for the Bell shares, threatening suit if the stock was not returned to him. Coleman ignored the threat. On August 9, Gordon made still another suggestion: Coleman should sell Feuerstein 600 shares and he, Gordon, would sell him 400 shares so "the concern will stand: Coleman 3,400; Gordon 3,600; Feuerstein 1,000." This, too, was refused.

Coleman was also writing firm letters to Gordon. For example, on August 22, he wrote admonishing Gordon to keep out of the business part of the firm, while stating he would not interfere with Gordon's duties as manager of the refinery.

In the meantime, in July 1865, Gordon had brought suit against the San Francisco Sugar Refinery, claiming he had promissory notes, advanced in 1860, amounting to $158,000 plus interest. (The rate on one was $2\frac{1}{2}$ percent a month!) John T. Doyle, Gordon's attorney, disapproved of the suit. He wrote Gordon on June 29, 1865, to "either quit having law suits or pay closer attention to them," and again later he urged him to avoid litigation.

Then unexpectedly in August 1865 Coleman sold all his sugar stock for $200,000. The new shareholders were John T. Doyle, 100 shares; D. O. Mills, 500 shares; W. C. Ralston, 500 shares; R. Feuerstein, 1,000 shares; and Nicholas Luning, 1,000 shares. In addition, Gordon's associates took 550 shares in the refinery: Stanger Tate took 300 shares, and Bernard Callahan and Charles De Ro each took 125. These totaled 3,650 shares. Gordon held 4,350, a safe majority.

Shortly afterwards, on September 22, 1865, the new by-laws of the San Francisco and Pacific Sugar Refinery were published in a pamphlet in San Francisco, printed by Towne and Bacon. The trustees were William C. Ralston, the major factor in San Francisco's business life at that time, Nicholas Luning, one of the wealthiest men in the city, Charles De Ro, R. Feuerstein, William Hooper and Gordon. Gordon became president and continued as manager, Stanger Tate became commercial agent, and William Hooper became secretary. Gordon had won complete control of the refinery. The battle was over!

The difficulties with Coleman had not deterred Gordon from entering the refinery's sugar in an exhibit at the Mechanics' Fair in 1864. It received a premium award. The committee members examined the refinery itself and found it in a "high state of perfection." Apparently all planned construction had been completed. The committee report listed several small buildings that were not included in the articles already mentioned: three cooperage shops, two warehouses employing forty hands, a carpenter shop, a blacksmith shop, and gas works. Also listed were two reservoirs, each containing 150,000 gallons of water.

The next year, 1865, the refinery received a silver medal at the Mechanics' Fair, and the report stated, "This company made a splendid exhibit of refined sugar and syrups of their manufacture." Gordon's refinery had become one of the most important industries in San Francisco. In 1865, only six individuals and organizations had larger incomes and larger assessed personal property values. That same year Samuel Bowles, the well known author and newspaper publisher, included a short account of the refinery in his book *Across the Continent,* describing the highlights of his tour to the West.

Gordon meanwhile was continuing his activities in the Chamber of Commerce, attending meetings even during trying times. When, in 1865, the Art Institute, the forerunner of the present San Francisco Art Institute, opened rooms at 312 Montgomery Street with an "elegant collation," Gordon was listed as a subscriber.

On August 16, 1865, the Gordon family participated in a fashionable event, the marriage of Miss Julia Hort to George Chauncey Boardman. The ceremony was held in the "handsome new residence of the Horts at 729 Sutter Street." Nellie was a bridesmaid, as were Cora Lyon and Sue Throckmorton, daughters of important San Franciscans. Samuel Hort was an associate of the financial firm of C. Adolphe Low and Company, while George Boardman was president of the San Francisco Fire Insurance Company and later representative of the Aetna Insurance Company.

The Boardmans continued to be friends of George Gordon, for in Gordon's will he left shares in the Sugar Refinery to "Julia, wife of George Boardman."

That Gordon at this period was one of the best known men in San Francisco is evidenced by a poem written by Bret Harte in 1864, which appeared in the *Californian:*

SOUTH PARK
(After Gray)

The foundry tolls the knell of parting day,
   The weary clerk goes slowly home to tea,
The North Beach car rolls onward to the bay,
   And leaves the world to solitude and me.

Now fades the glimmering landscape on the sight,
   And through the Park a solemn hush prevails,
Save, in the distance, where some school-boy wight
   Rattles his hoop-stick on the iron rails;

Save, that from yonder jealous-guarded basement
   Some servant-maid vehement doth complain,
Of wicked youths who, playing near her casement,
   Project their footballs through her window-pane.

Can midnight lark or animated "bust"
   To these grave scenes bring mirth without alloy?
Can shrill street-boys proclaim their vocal trust
   In John, whose homeward march produces joy?

Alas! for them no organ-grinders play,
   Nor sportive monkey move their blinds genteel;
Approach and read, if thou canst read, the lay,
   Which these grave dwellings through their stones reveal:

"Here rests his fame, within yon ring of earth,
   A soul who strove to benefit mankind –
Of private fortune and of public worth,
   His trade – first man, then sugar he refined.

"Large was his bounty, and he made his mark;
   Read here his record free from stains or blots:
He gave the public all he had – his Park;
   He sold the public – all he asked – his lots!"

Europe

With his cane sugar refinery difficulties solved, Gordon had dreams of a new conquest, sugar beet refining.

Sugar beet history is short compared to sugar cane's two millenniums. Not until the eighteenth century was the presence of sugar in beets recognized. The pioneer beet-sugar factory was established in Silesia, and gradually others were built in Germany and France. By the middle of the nineteenth century the industry was well established in Europe.

It developed slowly in the United States, however. Early efforts resulted in failure. In 1852 the Mormons made the first attempt in the West to extract sugar commercially from beets. It was not successful. Nevertheless, within the next decade several attempts were made in San Francisco. In 1856 a coppersmith, Belper, built a small factory in Ocean View; it failed. Eugene Delessert exhibited sugar he had made at the first Industrial Exhibition of the Mechanics' Institute in 1857, but his enterprise was commercially unsuccessful. The San Jose Pioneer Beet Sugar Company, established in 1857, also came to naught. These attempts, and recurrent articles in the public press, however, indicate continuing interest in beet sugar. The Hungarian, Colonel Agoston Haraszthy, added to his famous 1862 book, *Grape Culture, Wines and Wine Making,* a nine-page article on sugar beets and the manufacture of sugar.

Gordon had apparently become interested in the subject by 1861, for, on September 22, the *Alta* carried a letter from a leading Napa Valley farmer, J. W. Osborn, suggesting that "a speedy way of ascertaining whether the culture of sugar beets for manufacturing purposes can be profitable, is for farmers in different parts of the state, who have raised sugar beets the present season, to send, say, one-half a dozen specimens to George Gordon at the Sugar Refinery with a letter of location, soil (etc.) with the object to find the amount of saccharine contained."

Gordon replied in a letter to the *Alta* a few days later. He stated that the San Francisco Sugar Refinery would "undertake to send each parcel in air-exhausted glass bottles to Europe for analysis." If reports were favorable, he added, he might "be a large purchaser of beet juice."

In 1865 Gordon himself went to Europe. On October 18, accompanied by his wife and daughter, he sailed on the *Golden Age.*

"George Gordon will inspect the sugar refineries of Europe and the United States," noted a contemporary newspaper. "Mr. Gordon has labored energetically for years in the development of the resources of the Pacific, and few men are as capable of presenting the progress we have made to the people of other states."

The trip was to last two years and include travel, frustration and illness on the part of Gordon, and homesickness on the part of his wife and daughter.

Most of the Gordon letters that have survived are business letters. However, at the California State Library is a collection of forty-three letters, which the Gordons wrote to John T. Doyle during this trip. These relate in part to business, but they are also personal letters to a friend. Bancroft Library has some of Doyle's replies.

The family had gone first to England, then to France. In a letter of February 13, 1866, from Paris, Gordon praised the French capital as his "beau ideal of a City." He contrasted the food with England's. "I was almost starved with hunger in England," but "I am now of the opinion that the only cooking worth knowing is the French."

London itself he had found "too crowded . . . too sombre and dingy . . . its people too serious and solid to be agreeable." He had been ill, he wrote, but had improved enough to be able to ride horseback in Paris with his daughter. He praised her horsemanship: "Nell was splendid, mounted on an English hunter . . . she managed it with a firm hand and was in my estimation at least by far the finest equestrian in the Bois."

He was less pleased with affairs at home. "I am greatly annoyed at the action of that fool, Spreckles," he wrote (misspelling the name of the future West Coast sugar king) "in building another sugar refinery for which there is no room." Claus Spreckels had recently organized and became manager of the Bay Sugar Company, located at Union and Battery Streets.

Gordon also informed Doyle in the same letter, "I saw I. C. Woods lately in London where he conveyed the lots to me and that is all that is wanted." Woods was a brother-in-law of Robert Emmett Doyle, as well as a business associate of the Doyles. Apparently Woods had left unfinished business when he had fled from San Francisco ten years earlier after the failure of Adams and Company Express, the company he had headed.

Writing again from Paris two months later, Gordon suggested to Doyle that he attempt to sell for him 1,500 shares of his refinery stock at $70 per share, although he was of the opinion that its actual worth was $75 a share. Gordon wrote that during the last five months of 1865 the profits of the refinery were $103,126; 2½ per cent per month. He continued that he had "too many eggs in one basket," and was "by habit always peering into the future," that it was "to my peace of mind to have a little division of risks." He advised Doyle to invest the proceeds of the sale in good stock. He also wrote he was considering placing $100,000 into beet sugar in California," but wished to investigate further. Gordon concluded, "I know more of sugar than any of its [California's] capitalists."

Nellie, on July 6, wrote from Geneva of their travels to Frankfurt, Baden-Baden, Heidelberg, Strasbourg, Basel, Lake Constance and Lucerne. She mentioned that the Fourth of July had been "celebrated in the usual manner by all good Americans."

Two days later, still in Geneva, Mrs. Gordon wrote how pleased she was that her husband's health had improved. "I think it is the absence of cares that will benefit him.   .   .   When he first came over he worked as hard as ever and I was fairly tired with the sound of beet root sugar.   .   .   He sticks to his little sweetheart, Nellie, as much as ever, they are always happy and contented together."

Gordon's "absence of cares" had, however, vanished by July 12. The Gordons were back in London, and Nellie wrote, "I think he has turned himself into a char machine and turns his steam on us to keep us from stagnating."

On July 28 Gordon wrote Doyle that he was not ready to return, but he gave much business advice. He suggested building a fireproof warehouse for the refinery in order to get "rid of town storage and cartage."

He also wished the refinery to sell its Bay Sugar Refinery stock, since his group had failed to gain control of the Spreckels enterprise and thus had no influence over it. Gordon also mentioned that obtaining information pertaining to sugar and refining was "slow work . . . you have to tread delicately and angle for invitations to visit refineries."

The difficulty he had in obtaining information regarding European methods of refining sugar became general knowledge. The English visitor to California, J. E. Player-Frowd, wrote in his *Six Months in California* (published in London in 1872): "The whole of the town south of Market is one entire plain, in the centre of which rises a large sugar bakery, built by an Englishman of the name of Gordon. He made an extended tour in Europe, visiting the various refineries. The managers of all are exceedingly jealous of strangers, so that Mr. G. had great difficulty in obtaining admission, and when in, could not even make a scratch with his pencil. He retained everything in his head, however, till he got to his hotel, when all was written down."

Referring to the rival Bay Sugar Refinery, Gordon wrote Doyle that Spreckels had placed his factory on the water's edge and "with moderate expense could convert it into a beet refinery where the beets could come by boats." Gordon suggested the possibility of changing the San Francisco Sugar Refinery into a "beet sugar house." He suggested if Doyle did sell all or part of Gordon's refinery stock as requested, he should buy stock in Ralston's Bank of California.

Later that same month, Gordon wrote from Nottingham commenting on Ralston's ideas for improving the financial condition of the refinery, which Doyle must have conveyed to him: "His [Ralston's] fertility of invention, so to speak, is enormous and if he could, like Napoleon, command the foremost talent in the world to nurse into strength and then to guide and govern the creation of his brain, it would be a different thing – but it will be probably disastrous for any of our people to take charge of his ideas and bring them forth. It would be like a mascular [*sic*] giant impregnating a female dwarf – the germ might be perfect in itself, but the mother would burst as it grew in her keeping. . . He must not judge our agents' capacity by his own."

On September 7, Gordon wrote from Glasgow that reports indicated a loss for the refinery of $45,516 for the first six months, but that he believed it would run to $70,000. He strongly advised that the refinery stop selling sugar at a loss; he counseled that the way to control the market was not by buying stock in the Bay Sugar Refinery, but by reducing the costs of producing sugar. He explained that "Bay and Spreckles [*sic*] are weak and ignorant of their business, better opponents than new men." He was still in poor health and explained that the "muddle in San Francisco makes me worse," but he could not return home "until I find how they can refine sugar at one-third less than it costs us for the same thing."

Ill health continued to plague Gordon and on September 24, 1866, Mrs. Gordon wrote to Doyle from Glasgow "if anything happens to him, I fancy they would all go wrong." She noted, "Nellie presently is in the hands of an Aurist "trying to cure her deafness."

During the month of October the family visited Nottingham, Manchester and Clifton. On October 13 Gordon wrote, "If I can ever get out of this cursed country . . . We are all dreadfully homesick .

. . so now, as the good Catholics do for their spiritual welfare, I propose for my corporal, to go into retreat."

On November 27, writing from Clifton, a spa noted for its hot springs, Gordon declared himself a Californian and reported that "Mrs. Gordon and Nell are the most desolate homesick people you ever saw, they are positively weary and disgusted with England." He described the English working men as "bleary, mutton-brained, lumpish fellows on the main" compared to "intelligent educated Yankee boys." Noted Gordon, "That England occupies the place she does is due to the educated middle classes" – incidentally, precisely the class from which the Gordons sprang.

His wife's homesickness is certainly at variance with the allegation in Gertrude Atherton's legend that she wished to live in England. Mrs. Gordon wrote a most revealing letter from Clifton on December 1, the contents of which are further in conflict with the legend. Her handwriting and her style certainly were not those of an uneducated bar maid. Nor do any of her letters indicate family hatred.

She wrote to Doyle regarding her husband's health that "when things go wrong, he gets pulled down again. . . You ask what Nellie and I are doing – I can answer you in one word – nothing. We came over to this part of the world I thought to travel and improve our minds by observation of manners and customs of different countries, but since the month of July we have been completely stagnated. Then we don't like England nor the English, consequently when we had seen our relatives, who are now reduced to very few, we were anxious to be off to some more congenial place, where we should meet Americans or even Irishmen. Instead G.G. drags us all round to these business places, where we never see a soul from one day to another. . . We were six weeks in Glasgow – the dreariest town I was ever in – and we have been nearly the same time here. When you go out, you meet ancient and decayed old men and women, drawn about in Bath chairs, trying to keep themselves alive. I think the English Spa towns are horrible. G.G. is working himself old and haggard, but tries to make himself youthful by shaving off his beard, wearing a blue cravat and carrying a stick. He gets up every morning and lights the fire at ½ past 5, makes himself some tea and writes until breakfast time, then goes out. We do not see him until night."

As for Nellie, "poor child, she is getting quite sad and lonely over here – with no beaus, no dances."

On December 4 Gordon wrote Doyle that his wife and "Nell" had gone to Nice for a month. He also defended Ralston's bank: "Those attacks of the 'American Flag' on the Bank of California should be consigned to the devil – why can't they be prosecuted?" Gordon probably still remembered with distaste the newspaper's attack upon him.

A month later, in January 1867, he wrote from Paris that he had had a visit from California financier A. A. Cohen regarding Alameda railroad lands. A few days later he was back in England, and a letter from Bristol indicates his health was poor and that he did not wish to make the trip to California, as he would have to return to Europe later. He also wished to see the Paris International Exposition.

From Milan on March 16, he wrote Doyle stating he had "little if any improved in health. . . I think I was improving somewhat till I got to Rome, when I caught the miserable fever which haunts that miserable place. The energetic spirit of our party is Mrs. G. She was bent on seeing the Pope and sure enough saw him and all the Cardinals except Antonelli. . . In the Coliseum, which she faithfully visited, her greatest admiration was for some chickens which were scratching in the arena and were better than ours at Mayfield Grange. . . We have just come from Venice, a nasty mildewed place and have got to Milan, which is bright, clean, thrifty, as handsome a city as you would wish to see."

They continued travel from March through May on the Continent, returning to England the end of June.

Doyle had been urging Gordon to return to San Francisco, even writing to Nellie asking her to use her influence. On June 20 Doyle wrote that De Ro had become alarmed and that Stanger Tate, who was acting manager of the refinery in Gordon's absence, had been "left too long without Gordon's eye; without Gordon's vigilance the whole business tends to slide."

Gordon reluctantly decided to return and arranged for passage. He advised Doyle he would arrive in San Francisco in September and asked him to engage a suite, "two chambers, parlor and bathroom," at the Lick, San Francisco's first great luxury hotel.

In the meantime, on June 12, there had been an important meeting of the stockholders of the Sugar Refinery. The need for additional capital was such that a resolution of Ralston's was passed unanimously: each shareholder would pay into the company $18.75 for each share owned. It was hoped $150,000 would be raised in this manner.

At that time the shares were distributed as follows: Gordon, 4,235, voted by De Ro his attorney in fact; Doyle, 150; De Ro, 125; Luning, 1,265; Feuerstein, 800; Ralston, 500; D. O. Mills, 500; Tate, 100; Bernard

Callahan (chief engineer of the refinery), 125; and Frederick Roeding, 200 shares. Gordon's holdings were about 53% of the shares. Informed of the resolution passed at the meeting, Gordon reacted unfavorably. He wrote Doyle that "my wife and I" had come to the conclusion that they did not wish to place any more funds in the refinery.

On July 17 he wrote that his health was such that he should not cross "the tropics or plains" in August, and that he must return to England to protect his patents; he had been offered $10,000 for one. Nevertheless, on July 27 the Gordon family finally sailed from Liverpool on the steamship *Russia*.

On August 5 Gordon was writing from New York that he very much regretted "having to make this long hasty journey simply to do what I could have done back there" in Europe. Nevertheless, he informed Doyle, "Will drop everything and sail, Saturday, August 10 – say nothing except to De Ro."

The Gordons reached Panama in time to sail for San Francisco on August 19 on the steamer *Golden City*. There were 498 passengers including 200 troops. Among the prominent passengers were William Alvord, later president of the Bank of California and mayor of San Francisco, and J. O. Eldridge, a former business associate of De Ro. W. F. Lapidge was captain and, more pertinent to this story, the ship's surgeon was Dr. C. C. Gordon, a native of Florida, not then but later related to George Gordon.

On September 1, 1867, the Gordons were home in San Francisco. Their arrival was not a pleasant homecoming, for it was followed shortly by the flight of Stanger Tate.

The Flight of Stanger Tate

While in Europe Gordon had been plagued by even more than ill health and the inability to obtain information regarding European methods of sugar refining. Increasingly worrisome reports had come to him about the misconduct of Stanger Tate, the man he had left in charge of the refinery.

Tate was an Englishman who had been associated with the refinery since 1859. He had served as a clerk, foreman, cashier and finally, when Gordon left for Europe, as "Deputy Manager."

As early as July 1866 warnings about Tate's behavior must have been conveyed to the Gordons, as Mrs. Gordon wrote on the eighth, "I am sorry there has been any trouble with Mr. Tate. I fancy George is mistaken, for I can hardly think Tate would be such a goose as to speculate in the mines when he knows the penalty."

On July 28 Gordon wrote suggesting to Doyle that Tate be watched and that a new manager was needed, one with "more drive than Tate." A few days later he added, "I am very much afraid there is more wrong than appears on the surface."

In October, Gordon thought he had found an excellent replacement for Tate; however, he wrote subsequently that they had "lost that gentleman." He also wrote, "I am puzzled about Tate, for instance he had never written to his mother since I have been away, although she has written every month."

On May 28, 1867, Gordon again expressed his displeasure regarding Tate and also referred to an earlier indication of Tate's gambling proclivities: "It is needless to say how grieved and incensed I am at the conduct of the man whom I took up as discharged from the United States Army and have befriended and borne with in every way since . . . and for whom I bought 300 shares to hold for three years on condition he would be faithful to his business and abstain from gambling."

Less than two weeks later, Gordon wrote Doyle advising that Tate be suspended; that while he had aided him in a former escapade when he lost $3,000 gambling, he would not again do so. Doyle informed Gordon the same month that Tate was drinking, that his "face, red, does not look well."

The alarmed Gordon decided to hurry home. En route, he wrote from New York that Tate's "brain is turned or he has something to be covered." He arrived in San Francisco to find a disaster far more serious than he anticipated.

The front page of the *Alta* on September 7, 1867, six days after Gordon's return, carried a headline, "One More Unfortunate." The article below it read: "It is rumored on the street that the cashier of one of our largest manufacturing establishments has levanted, that is to say, left on the *Great Republic,* having lost an immense sum, some say as much as $100,000.00, by gambling within a few months. There is nothing positively known on the subject and we do not give the name for that reason."

The name was Stanger Tate!

Later that day the *Evening Bulletin* gave details: "Serious Defalcation" – "One of those unfortunate circumstances which from time to time throw commercial circles into consternation, plunge the friends of the guilty into grief, and bring eternal disgrace on his innocent relatives has just come to light. It appears Stanger Tate . . . has defrauded the Company of between $75,000.00 and $100,00.00. Mr. Gordon arrived by the steamer on Sunday and went to the Refinery to meet Mr. Tate, but either by accident or design, Tate kept out of his way, not only on that day, but on the following day. On Tuesday, Tate left by the *Great Republic,* getting a friend to drive him to the steamer, but not telling him he was going. His young wife, an amiable lady with two children, had no idea that her husband had done wrong or even that there was any trouble on his mind, until she learned that he had fled the country. . . Gambling with men of greater means than himself is said to have been the cause of his crime."

On September 7 the *San Francisco Times* added further information on Tate's departure. Its long article reads in part: "Further investigations were at once made and it is now generally believed that the defaulter took his departure for China or Japan on board the steamer *Great Republic* which sailed on Tuesday last. . . It is said that Tate was addicted to gambling and that this runious passion was the immediate cause of the catastrophe. It has been known for some time that he played high, and it was suspected that he was losing. . . It is presumed that he had been fleeced of nearly everything by the gamblers. . . He has always borne a very high character among business men until recently, but within the past few months he had taken to drinking, and was altogether leading a rather fast life. . . Probably the knowledge of his danger impelled him to the immoderate use of stimulants. . .

The case is another argument for the suppression of gambling."

The *Alta* on September 8, under the heading of "A Victim of a Draw," had lurid details: "It is now positively asserted that Stanger Tate . . . is actually a defaulter to the extent of $75,000 to $100,000." He had been "fleeced out" at "draw poker" and the "players are known."

The next day the paper carried a report that the sugar company maintained that the amount of the deficit was exaggerated. The *Bulletin* scaled the sum down, stating that it "may reach from $10,000 to $15,000."

In sailing out of the Golden Gate one jump ahead of the sheriff, Tate was following the course of Harry Meiggs and I. C. Woods, both previously mentioned. He was not the last of these gifted but unstable characters to flee through the Gate, as in 1886 Charles W. Banks, trusted cashier of Wells Fargo and Company absconded, sailing to far away Rarotonga, in the Cook Islands.

Some two and a half months after Tate's flight the affair was again in the news. The *Bulletin* of November 21, 1867, had a detailed account: "Stanger Tate on His Travels – the Story of Confidence Operations on a Grand Commercial Scale." It related Tate's absconding, and discussed the large amount believed lost, and the company's treatment of the affair as a "trivial matter." The *Bulletin* claimed that "those who knew Tate, his position in the Refinery, his great business capacity, his social popularity, his style of living, and his personal credit, did not believe he had thrown this all away and committed a criminal act through the pressure of a trivial debt of $5,000. . . Stanger Tate had more than one friend who would endorse his note for that sum. Had he remained two days longer, he would have become the possessor of $1,000.00 by a bet on the election." The newspaper claimed politics was a causative factor. It reported that Tate, who was an active member of the Democratic County Convention, had remarked "how glad he was to get away from the political excitement," alleging that "politics make a man drink more than is good for him."

The account told how, after the ship had passed through the Gate, Tate appeared and was greeted warmly by friends who were passengers. He informed them that Gordon had sent him "to look up the sugar market" in Manila and Batavia. Among those greeting him cordially were Commodore James Watkins and Cornelius Koopmanschap, a prominent San Francisco commission and insurance agent. Tate was careful not to gamble or drink excessively, the article continued, and reported that he apparently had ample means, the purser stating he had $2,000. "No one guessed from his manner that he had left a wife to bear alone an agony of shame worse than death, and prattling children who must be told never again to speak his name."

The steamer called at Yokohama, then went on to Hong Kong where Koopmanschap "introduced Tate to his partner and made him free of the Club." Tate became "well known in the best set." Oliphant and Company, agents for the Sugar Refinery, "prevailed upon him to take his abode with them." Tate engaged a ship "to go to Manila and load sugar for San Francisco," and "another vessel was sent to Batavia to load sugar for the same destination." Ten days after his arrival in Hong Kong, after a farewell dinner, Tate left for Singapore. Among his traveling companions was "Mr. Pierce of the firm of Peele, Hubbell and Company of

Manila. . . Pierce was very attentive to Tate, hoping to obtain the agency of the great sugar company for his firm."

When the ship *China* arrived later at Hong Kong with the news that their honored guest was a defaulter and absconder, there was "a great sensation in the best circles."

The *San Francisco Times* of November 22 repeated the Hong Kong banquet story and concluded that "no doubt the Hong Kong merchants will be extremely gratified when they learn upon whom they have been lavishing their hospitality."

The Sugar Refinery reacted to these stories by having De Ro, as its commercial agent, write a letter to the newspapers. The front page of the *Alta* on November 22, referred to the "sensational accounts in the *Bulletin*" and called attention to the fact that it was publishing a letter of De Ro's. De Ro explained that when Gordon left for Europe, Tate had become deputy manager and as such was merely in charge of the mechanical part of the business; that Tate never was agent or commercial agent; that he never held power of attorney or signed checks. Tate had robbed the company by fraudulent bills for supplies. He was aware that upon Gordon's return his action would be discovered so he absconded without ever seeing Gordon. The drafts against the firm given to Borman and Company amounted to $2,000, and to Oliphant and Company, $1,500, De Ro explained. These sums totaled considerably less than some of the newspaper reports. De Ro's letter to the public was an attempt by the refinery to minimize the whole affair; however, some of De Ro's statements are not completely correct. Tate held more power while Gordon was away than De Ro implied. The fact that the value of the refinery's stock declined and never regained its 1865 high suggests that the losses due to Tate's depredations were indeed quite large.

In 1865, before leaving San Francisco for his European tour, Gordon had made a will that named Tate as one of the possible executors of his estate in case his wife predeceased him. The will also asked that "Stanger Tate and his wife Agnes Tate" be taken care of. While in Europe, Gordon still retained some regard for Tate, writing as late as July 17, 1867, "I don't want to hurt him a feather's worth." However, after he returned to San Francisco and became aware of the amount of the embezzlement, his attitude changed. On September 6, 1867, Gordon signed a codicil to his will revoking the provisions naming Tate.

A final report on Tate came years later. In October 1886, John T. Doyle testified before the Superior Court of Santa Clara County in the matter of the estate of George Gordon. Doyle told of "one Stanger Tate who fled from this state about twenty years since, and whom the last I heard was that he was suffering imprisonment under a conviction of forgery in England." Such was the fate of Tate!

The Final Years

George Gordon, in California once more, re-entered the business and civic life of San Francisco with characteristic energy. He set about repairing his own business affairs as well. On November 6, 1867, little more than two months after his return from Europe, he could write to Ralston, "I see daylight." He explained that the refinery now owed money only to Ralston's Bank of California and to the Pacific and Union Insurance Company. He had already paid off $100,000, and he expected to pay $200,000 to the bank in December and January. He reported that the Bay Sugar Company and Spreckels representatives were having frequent quiet talks with him regarding controlling excess production. He asked Ralston's support for his plan to move the "books and checks" from 215 Front Street in downtown San Francisco to the Refinery, explaining, "I want them under my eye." In this same letter Gordon also expressed his belief that De Ro, Feuerstein and Roeding were required by "law and commercial honour" to aid in repaying his company's losses in the matter of the "Tate stealings" as they "permitted" them to take place.

Feuerstein expressed his contrary views just before he left for Europe the following spring. By then, his association with the refinery had ended. From New York, he wrote Ralston a long emotional letter in which he reported he had left San Francisco "in an irritated and most unpleasant state of mind," embittered "after such a long and satisfactory career." He appeared to believe Ralston supported Gordon in blaming him for negligence in the Tate affair. On returning from Honolulu in October 1867, Feuerstein continued, he was "thunderstruck" by Tate's "defalcation." Gordon's "charges" against him were told to him by De Ro and Roeding, and he recalled that Ralston had advised him to "keep cool . . . the matter would blow over."

Defending his actions concerning Tate and the management of the refinery, he explained that he had considered Tate a "partner or colleague" not "a clerk;" that it "might have been wiser to place less confidence in men, but nobody would charge culpability;" and that an individual would be judged by "his character" and not by the "number of dollars involved and the legal points of the case."

Ralston was disturbed by this letter and sent it to Roeding with a note saying: "You see Friend Feuerstein has given an entirely improper construction to my views." He called Gordon's efforts to obtain reimbursement from Feuerstein "that cursed business" and added that he wished "to end the matter."

Following the Tate affair, the management of the sugar refinery changed. In 1867 Gordon had been listed in the City Directory as "manager" and Feuerstein as "commercial agent." No president was given. The trustees were Luning, Feuerstein, Ralston, Tate, De Ro, and W. Hooper, who was also the trustees' secretary. In 1868 and 1869, Gordon was listed as president, while no agent or secretary was given. The trustees had changed; Luning, Ralston and De Ro remained, but the other three, Tate, Hooper and Feuerstein were replaced by two, John T. Doyle and Frederick Roeding.

The refinery was still listed as having capital of

$800,000.00. The newspapers listed it as one of the major taxpayers of the city; and it was still the leading California producer of sugar, employing 130 men to Spreckels' 60. Gordon's refinery, in fact, still claimed to be the "largest sugar refinery in the United States."

Its affairs continued to be of general interest. On September 17, 1868, the *Alta* reported that $100,000 worth of sugar being shipped from Hawaii to Gordon's refinery had been seized by customs officers. It was alleged to be adulterated by charcoal to make it appear to be lower grade than it really was. The San Francisco *News Letter* on September 26 claimed the sugar was made to look dirty so as to require less tax. Gordon, as usual, was quick to defend himself in letters to the press. In a letter to the *Alta* he denied in eight points any guilt in the matter and alleged that the seizure was made because the customs officers and the consul in the Sandwich Islands received one half of all property seized.

Regardless of his many difficulties, Gordon carried on his duties as before. For example, he exhibited at the 1868 Mechanics' Fair; the *News Letter* commented on the "tasteful arrangement" of his sugar products. A pleasant interlude was reported in the same publication May 24, 1868, under the caption "Picnic at Menlo Park." Gordon had invited the employees of the refinery with their families and friends to a picnic "at his beautiful country seat" in honor of Mrs. Gordon's birthday. A special train brought four hundred persons to Mayfield Grange. After a "bounteous collation," the "multitude" listened to the "delicious strains of the band" until four o'clock. Then John T. Doyle, "in a few well chosen remarks proposed three cheers for the President's estimable lady. . . These were given in rousing style and were followed by three each for Mr. Gordon himself and his beautiful and accomplished daughter; to which Mr. G. responded in his particularly felicitous style."

Gordon also continued to speak out regarding public affairs. In November 1867 the Chamber of Commerce called a special meeting to discuss the proposed Reciprocity Treaty between the United States and the monarchy of Hawaii. There was opposition to this treaty on the ground that anything that would enrich the Islands would strengthen the monarchy and thus defer annexation by the United States.

Gordon spoke in favor of the treaty. He believed if duties were lowered by the treaty, there would be an increased production of sugar cane in Hawaii and an influx of American residents. This would result in the Islands becoming more American than Hawaiian and pave the way for them to become part of the United States. He compared the policy to that of England in obtaining the Channel Islands and the United States proposal to purchase territory on the Island of Borneo for a shipping base. He held that the United States' acquisition of outlying territory would deprive enemies of places where they could "recruit and take refuge." He urged support of the treaty for the benefits it would bring to California. At the conclusion of the meeting Gordon was appointed chairman of a committee to study the subject and make recommendations to the Chamber.

The following month the committee submitted its report. Not surprisingly, it asked the Chamber to support the treaty. The report not only favored the acquisition of the Hawaiian Islands but also British Columbia! The committee suggested that when the proposed treaty expired in the 1874-1875 legislative year, economic conditions would be such that the Islands would have to join the United States. Although one committee member objected on the ground that the treaty would strengthen the monarchy, the majority report was finally accepted by the Chamber in a close vote: 15 yes, 13 no.

The United States Senate, however, rejected the treaty. Not until a decade later was a Treaty of Reciprocity finally negotiated. This was followed, as Gordon had predicted, by the immediate extension of the sugar industry. The Islands entered into what the English author Noel Deerr called an "American Zollverein," a union for maintenance of a common tariff, leading to the political union of 1898.

In 1868 San Francisco experienced a severe smallpox epidemic, and Gordon injected his ideas into a campaign to control that dreaded disease. The first cases appeared in March. By June, 153 had been reported. The death rate was appalling – 20 in June, then steadily increasing to 97 in November and 148 in December. San Francisco was a city in panic. On December 11, the *Alta* reported the proceedings of a smallpox meeting held at the Merchants Exchange. Gordon submitted four resolutions to be adopted and forwarded to the city supervisors. He urged the following program:

(1) Vaccinations.
(2) House-to-house inspection in each district by a physician in charge of the area.
(3) Rigid isolation of the infected.
(4) Strict supervision of all students in the schools by competent personnel.

As an example of the kind of abuse that should be corrected, Gordon reported that a man with smallpox lay in a lot on Folsom Street for a day before being taken to a hospital.

The meeting adjourned after a committee was appointed to make further investigation. Again George Gordon was named chairman. The other members were A. A. Cohen and Dr. Augustus J. Bowie, the latter a prominent physician.

Dr. Isaac Rowell, the city's health officer, stated publicly that vaccination had little effect. He favored the use of chlorine and fumigation. The San Francisco Medical Society debated the treatment and prevention of this great plague at their meetings during November and December 1868 and January 1869. Viewing the controversy a century later, one finds the clearest statements were made by Dr. Henry Gibbons and his son Dr. Henry Gibbons, Jr. In the *Pacific Medical and Surgical Journal,* of which they were "editors and proprietors," they urged vaccination and also a newer idea, re-vaccination. They labeled false the currently held views that the epidemic was increasing because of a cessation of the sea breezes, and that the use of carbolic acid, the cleaning of the sewers and improvement of the Department of Public Health would be of benefit. The Gibbons reiterated that universal vaccination was the preventative.

The heroic work of the Sisters of Mercy during that smallpox epidemic will always be remembered by a grateful city. In August 1868 they offered their services to the stricken citizens. The offer was accepted, and as the epidemic increased, an emergency frame hospital was hurriedly built in the Potrero not far from the present City Hospital. The Sisters staffed the Smallpox Hospital until the epidemic finally subsided in May 1869. It is the tradition that because of this service, the privilege of free transportation on the city streetcars was given the Sisters. It continues to this day.

Earthquakes also engaged George Gordon's interest in this period. On August 13 and 14, 1868, there was a great earthquake in Peru; in Arequipa alone more than 500 persons were killed. When news of this disaster reached San Francisco, a relief committee was established and funds were solicited. The San Francisco and Pacific Sugar Refinery was one of the larger donors, contributing $100.

Later in 1868 San Francisco was also the victim of an earthquake. On October 21 there were severe temblors along the Hayward Fault across the Bay. There was considerable damage in San Francisco and five persons were killed. The buildings of South Park were not damaged, but the Sugar Refinery's chimney "was broken off and fell to the ground," according to the *Alta* of October 22. It reported that "a number of workingmen were on the point of going out of the building into the yard when the chimney fell." Fortunately, none was injured.

His attention caught, Gordon pursued the subject with more letters to the public press. Ten days after the earthquake, the *News Letter* published an exceedingly lengthy communication headed "Earthquake-proof Houses." Gordon began it," Allow me to say a word or two. . ." and ended by writing over two thousand! He praised wood and condemned brick construction. He wrote in detail regarding structures to be built on filled ground, always the most susceptible to damage.

Shortly after, on November 6, Gordon wrote another detailed letter on earthquakes to James Otis, President of the Chamber of Commerce. It was published in the *Alta* on November 11. He described two brick buildings side by side on man-made ground. One, the

Gas Works, lay in ruins after the recent earthquake. The other, a part of the Vulcan Iron Works, remained intact. Gordon stated his belief that constructing buildings that would withstand earthquakes was "simply a matter of cost." He urged that studies be made at once before the recent events were forgotten.

"Our citizens subscribed $15,000 for relief in Peru," he wrote, "let us subscribe $10,000 to aid in preventing suffering in our midst from the same cause. There is less eclat in prevention than in relief, but it is a more substantial service to keep heads from being broken than to give plaster to mend them when fractured." The Chamber, he urged, should administer the fund, and he offered to subscribe $100 toward it himself.

He also urged the Chamber to advocate laws which would prevent "careless or niggardly property owners from jeopardizing the lives and property of their neighbors by erecting or maintaining tumble-down edifices." He concluded, "We, in effect, say to the Earthquake, 'You came on us unawares and we confess shook our nerves; but in reply we throw down the gauntlet to you – give us time to investigate you and you may move on our works'."

Gordon's suggestions bore fruit. On November 25, the *Alta* reported that the Chamber of Commerce had held an "Earthquake Committee" meeting. Gordon had read the program of the projected study to be undertaken by five sub-committees. Their fields of inquiry were implied in their names:

(1) On Bricks, Stones and Timber.
(2) On Limes, Cements, and other Bonds and Braces.
(3) On Structural Designs.
(4) Scientific Inquiry and Collection of Facts.
(i.e. the force and direction of earthquakes)
(5) Legal; Law Governing Buildings.

THE BUILDING OF I. FRIEDLANDER AT SANSOME AND CALIFORNIA STREETS
Constructed in 1870 on the northeast corner, using Gordon's earthquake-resistant
plans. It was not damaged by the 1906 quake but the following fire destroyed it.
On the northwest corner, at left, was Ralston's Bank of California building.

Courtesy of the Wells Fargo Bank History Room.

Gordon was elected president of the Earthquake Committee.

Both the committee and the sub-committees set to work quickly, meeting frequently. On December first Gordon explained to the committee the measures used to strengthen the refinery building; it was being anchored and bound together by iron rods. He also reported that of his two wooden houses at Menlo Park, the one anchored to the foundation had not suffered any damage, while the other, not attached to the foundations, had shaken so that plates and other articles were thrown from the shelves.

At another meeting four days later, Doyle suggested that the Mission records be searched for earthquake information. At the same time it was announced that two distinguished scholars had been added to the committee. They were physician and author Dr. J. D. B. Stillman, and Professor George Davidson, an eminent scientist.

The *News Letter,* reporting iconoclastically on this December 5 meeting, commented, "This honorable body of fossils are heavy on dignity and caution" and suggested a simple solution. The "best plan for bracing up old rattletrap concerns around town, that ought to tumble down by ordinary gravitation" would be to "tear down the shanties that are only waiting for a shake to tumble them down on our heads."

This ridicule was typical of the *News Letter* and its pugnacious founder and editor, Frederick Marriott. "Gentlemen of the Earthquake Investigation Committee you have made yourselves ridiculous," it charged on January 2, 1869. Referring to Gordon it asked, "Is none of your white sugar brown under the top layer?" On January 16 it addressed a letter to "Dear George" under the caption "A Sweet Chiding." It claimed Gordon had at first suggested definite building rules to prevent earthquake damage, only to later state, "The results . . . so far are wholly preliminary." It continued, "But the greatest error of all, dear George, was not pointing out to you your preeminent fitness for an exclusively sugarly lot – a solely saccharine existence." It added the hope that "the next earthquake . . . may find you with hands glued to the honest ladle, stirring that sugar."

The work of the Earthquake Committee was not wasted, however, nor was George Gordon's contribution. For example, I. Friedlander in 1870 erected a building at the north-east corner of California and Sansome. The 1870 City Directory praised it for its solidity and safety as well as its beauty, and a newspaper article noted that it was "built according to the late George Gordon's earthquake proof plan." That Gordon's plan worked is proved by photographs of this building taken after the 1906 earthquake. No damage is visible. It was, however, destroyed by the fire that followed.

Nellie Gordon was frequently in the news during these years. In contrast to her social isolation in Europe was her activity at home. On January 22, 1868, she was among the guests at a ball at Mrs. Barron's mansion. Her costume was described as "white lavender striped silk, trimmed with Cluny silk," and the press added a quotation to describe Nellie:

> With eyes whose beams might shame a
> night of starlight gleam,
> they were so bright.

On October 14 of the same year, Nellie was a guest at a party given by Miss Matilda Ann Ransome, daughter of the Leander Ransomes and sister of the social chronicler Amelia Ransome Neville. "Miss Gordon wore a buff with white silk, in which she looked nice enough to eat," recorded the press admiringly, again adding a quotation:

> There's a danger in that
> dazzling eye,
> That woos one with its witching
> smile.

Nellie also continued her riding and in 1867 regained, after a suit, her sorrel mare, sired by I. C. Wood's famous Kentucky stallion, "Peacock."

Gordon's interest in the St. Andrew's Society also continued. While he was born in England, and his parents were married, buried, and spent at least the major part of their lives in England, they apparently had a Scottish background. Certainly Gordon never corrected the general impression that he was a Scotsman. In November 1867 the St. Andrews Society's annual banquet scheduled Gordon to speak on "The Day We Honor," referring to November 30, the feast day of the Patron of Scotland and their society. The next year he spoke at the "sixth anniversary banquet" of the Society at the Lick Hotel on "Land o' Cakes." According to the *News Letter* of December 5, 1868, his remarks did not meet with favor. His patriotism for his adopted land led to a rebuke: "Although a Scotchman, he drew a somewhat unfavorable comparison between his native land and his adopted country. His remarks were considered ill timed and in bad taste and evidently offended the members present."

More acceptable was his recommendation early the following year regarding government purchase of Año Nuevo Island, on the San Mateo County coast, for a

lighthouse. The Chamber of Commerce was urging
that lighthouses be built to aid coast navigation, but in
the case of Año Nuevo, the purchase price of the land
was under dispute. The owners were asking the government to pay $25,000, which was considered excessive.
The Chamber appointed a committee to make recommendations as to a fair price. The members were J.
Mora Moss, Thomas Selby, and George Gordon – "all
eminent men," as Caspar T. Hopkins characterized
them in his account of the matter in his *Recollections.*

Their findings were submitted in February. The *Alta*
of February 18 reported that the committee had ini-
tially considered $10,000 as a fair price for the land
which, their report stated, "is entirely worthless for
agricultural purposes . . . a mass of rocks and
shingles." Gordon did not sign the report, but filed with
it was a letter from him, written in Menlo Park on
January 23, recommending that the government pay the
owners of Año Nuevo $12,000. The committee adopted
his figure, the Chamber adopted the report, and in 1870,
the Government purchased the island. It was to be the
last of many public issues in which George Gordon was
involved.

14

The Death of George Gordon

On February 24, 1869, Helen Mae Gordon, aged 24, married Dr. Charles Calhoun Gordon, aged 31. He had been the ship's surgeon aboard the Pacific Mail Steamship *Golden City* when Nellie and her family had returned to San Francisco from Europe two years earlier.

Born in Key West, Florida, Dr. Gordon had received his medical degree from the Long Island Hospital and Medical College in 1860. By the time of his marriage he had become a San Franciscan. He was serving as "physician and quarantine officer of the Port of San Francisco" and maintained an office at the northwest corner of Geary and Kearny streets.

The records of Trinity Church show that Nellie and Dr. Gordon were married by its pastor, the Reverend Christopher B. Wyatt. The witnesses of the ceremony were Mrs. George Gordon and J. D. Hambleton. Hambleton was an attorney, a partner of Dr. Gordon's brother, George W. Gordon, who practiced law in San Francisco.

Nellie's father had not attended the ceremony. His absence and the lack of any prior announcement of the marriage may be the reasons that it was considered an elopement. For example, an article in the *San Francisco Examiner* in 1880, "Brides and Bridals," stated, "Elopements have been very rare in San Francisco society. Still there have been instances which created a very great stir in society circles; being those of Miss

Lilly [*sic*] Hitchcock and Nellie Gordon." The famed
Lillie Hitchcock had married Howard Coit the same
year Nellie married, and against the wishes of both her
parents.

The informality of Nellie Gordon's marriage is indicated in the newspaper announcements which followed it; they carried the words "no cards." As
explained in the *San Francisco Elite Directory, 1879,*
the calling on the family of the bride "is a rigorous
formality," which apparently was not to be observed
in this instance.

George Gordon disliked his son-in-law intensely.
After the marriage his health steadily deteriorated, and
within three months he was dead. The Gordon legend
claimed he died of a "broken heart," and there appears
to be some evidence of the truth of this claim. However,
Gordon's letters from Europe disclosed his failing
health, as do letters from Doyle before the European
trip. But after Nellie's wedding he appeared to lose his
desire to live.

Doyle warned him in a letter: "You do yourself a
great injustice and weaken your position by allowing
Nellie's marriage to prey on your mind and affect your
conduct. The nice, true thing for you to do is to forgive
her – she is still nearer to you than all the rest of the
world. If you don't receive her back, you will never be
happy, nor she either. The general opinion of her husband is favorable . . . does not justify your harsh
judgment. You ought to try him."

The advice went unheeded. Gordon ceased attending
to refinery business with the result that Latham resigned as a trustee and Ralston threatened to take similar action. Doyle wrote to Gordon at Mayfield Grange
on March 18, 1869, that Roeding had been elected in

place of Latham, and added, "If you are sick and can't come to town, write me and I will try to come to you. . . . Your present course dejects your friends and your enemies exult."

Other problems presented themselves. On April 19 Doyle wrote the distressing news that "Luning told me Hale drinks, has been intoxicated in the office . . . we cannot keep him." Five days before, on April 14, 1869, Gordon had announced that he wished to resign from the presidency of the refinery. A letter of Latham's dated May 18 indicates Gordon's rapid decline. Addressed to his friend and business associate, George Wallace in Treasure City, Nevada, it concludes, "Old George Gordon is dying, will probably not live a week. Nellie's marriage fretted him sick. He has been sinking ever since."

On May 22 Gordon's illness reached the public press. The *Alta* reported, "An old and prominent citizen is dying at the Lick House. Last night he made his will and set his house in order for the impending change."

By the time the newspaper reached its readers, however, George Gordon was dead. That morning at seven, he had succumbed to what was recorded on his death certificate as pneumonia. "Old" George Gordon, as Latham termed him, was according to the newspapers, forty-nine years and eight months old. Actually, he was a year older, a not inconsiderable age in a time and place when longevity was not common.

The style of the newspapers of that period was to lavish praise on the deceased. However, few men were so lauded as Gordon. The *Herald's* obituary read in part: "George Gordon is dead! The announcement will come upon the community as unexpected and a heavy shock. For so much vitality as was compressed within that man's frame seemed so strong and large it would never die out, and so much intellect blazed from him in restless and incessant flashes, the quenching of it strikes us all with awe and wonderment. . . For, he was a good and honest man – intellect, to be sure, mastering everything in him . . . but with no lasting un-kindly hardness of nature withal. In George Gordon, death has robbed the City of San Francisco of one of her greatest citizens. No more active brain or brighter intellect ever busied itself with the advancement of the material interests of the city. In speaking and writing he had a persuasive eloquence that was exceedingly effective and his intercourse with his fellow men im-pressed them with a sense of his great power . . ." etc. The *Bulletin* carried a similar eulogy.

Gordon was described in an *Alta* news column as "a man of marked ability, wonderful energy, indom-itable perseverence and great decision of character . . . known and beloved for all those traits of char-acter which adorn the generous gentleman and noble-hearted citizen."

In an editorial, this same newspaper analyzed his character: "The death of George Gordon may be re-garded as a public calamity. He was one of the few clear-headed men who thoroughly comprehend the fact that individual success is bound up more or less in the success of the community in which he lives. He was public spirited in the largest and best sense of the term. The community is indebted to him for the dissemina-tion of the soundest ideas upon many questions. Em-inently practical, devoted as he was during his life to laying out, building up and organizing new enterprises, yet some of the productions of his pen manifested grace-ful writing, close reasoning and sound sense. If he had selected literary pursuits, he would unquestionably have achieved no ephemeral fame. . . He was almost fanatical in his democratic beliefs. . . He was essentially the man for a new country. . . But his brain was too powerful for the weak body. . . For some time past he had been wasting away slowly."

The San Francisco *News Letter* echoed this view, noting, "The fire of his intellect burnt so fiercely that it consumed him." And it reflected upon Gordon's life in more specific terms than had the other publications:

"Mr. Gordon had a great deal of what may be called the Benjamin Franklin ability – the faculty of devising means and expedients to accomplish useful ends, with the least expenditure of time and money. His administrative abilities were of a very high order, as evidenced by his successful management of various large industrial establishments, which, at various periods of his life he directed and controlled. Though essentially a practical man, he was well acquainted with modern literature, was familiar with history, and alive to the graces and beauty of poetry. Mr. Gordon was of a sociable disposition and when his mind was unbent from the cares and preoccupations of business, he delighted in gathering his friends around him and contributing to their enjoyment by his ready hospitality. Those who have experienced the kindness of Mr. Gordon and his family circle at Mayfield Grange will long retain vivid recollections of those pleasant reunions, and of the genial and kindly host; the central figure, who seemed never so happy as when diffusing happiness around him. . . A marked feature of Mr. Gordon's character was his kindness to the young. He was always ready to recognize and encourage youthful merit and was a marked favorite among young people of his acquaintance, who will mourn his loss."

Public response to Gordon's death was reported by the *Alta:* "Flags in respect to his memory were suspended at half-mast throughout Saturday. Special meetings of the Chamber of Commerce, British Benevolent Society and the St. Andrew's Society will be held . . . to make final arrangements to attend the funeral in bodies."

At the meeting of the Chamber of Commerce, James Otis, its president and later mayor of San Francisco, praised George Gordon, stating that he had "worked too hard for his health and broke down in the prime of life." On the motion of Caspar T. Hopkins, a resolution in honor of Gordon was passed.

The funeral was held on May 24. The pallbearers included De Ro, Latham, Boardman, Otis, William Barron, H. M. Hale and Ransome, all long-time associates of George Gordon. Also serving were two men from the refinery, James Hendren, clerk, and Bernard Callahan, chief engineer. Two additional pallbearers, new to the Gordon story, were Joseph A. Donohoe and Henry Barroilhet, wealthy and prominent men of affairs in the city.

The funeral cortege left the Lick Hotel at one o'clock, proceeding along Montgomery Street to Post, then west on Post to Gordon's church, Trinity, at Union Square. It was a long and impressive cortege. Two hundred and fifty employees of the refinery followed the hearse, as did members of the St. Andrews Society, the British Benevolent Society and the Chamber of Commerce. Following the marching units were over one hundred carriages bearing friends of the deceased. The church services were conducted by the Episcopal Bishop of California, the Right Reverend William Ingraham Kip.

After the ceremonies, Gordon was buried in Laurel Hill Cemetery. In 1940, when the bodies were moved from that location, those in the Gordon family plot were re-interred at Cypress Lawn Cemetery.

At N. Gray and Company, San Francisco's pioneer funeral parlor, the burial records are still preserved. George Gordon's physician was recorded as Jean Joseph Francois Haine, a Belgian-born physician with an extensive practice that included many members of prominent San Francisco families. The funeral expenses are also detailed at Gray's. They include payments for the choir of Trinity Church and for the hiring of eighty-three carriages and two omnibuses!

As noted, Gordon made his will in 1865, and after returning from Europe in 1867, changed it considerably. Both the 1865 will and the codicil of September 6, 1867, were signed at the Lick House. In the codicil, besides removing Stanger Tate and Tate's wife from his will, Gordon added that his sisters, Adamina Cockburn and Mary Cummings, were each to receive 100 shares of the refinery's stock. Also one Clementine Davis, who, when she presented her claim to the estate, was described as "single-divorced," received 100 shares; she was not a member of the household, and is not listed in the city directories. The daughter of Jane Potter, who let furnished rooms at 22 Kearny Street, was left 75 shares to be used for her education "at some Catholic school such as the convent at San Jose," Notre Dame Convent.

This youngster, Maud Potter, then five years old, was the subject of one of the later law suits in which the Gordon estate was involved. She apparently did not attend Notre Dame, but according to an account in the *Bulletin* of April 26, 1884, received her early education at Madam Forster's French Boarding School in San Francisco. In 1876 Maud was considered "qualified and of the proper age to be entered at the San Jose convent," according to John T. Doyle. However, her mother objected to her daughter leaving the city. Doyle then went to court, explaining that he had sold the stock left to Maud and had first loaned the money at interest and later invested it in Spring Valley Water Company stock. The value of the legacy had increased under his supervision. The Gordon heirs objected, stating that only the interest should go to Maud, that after her education the remaining sum should be returned to the estate. Judge Edward D. Wheeler ruled that Maud's education should continue in San Francisco until she was eighteen years old, and the balance of the capital should then go to her. Accordingly, Maud was placed in Madame Zeitska's Young Ladies Institute in the city.

In Gordon's will, Lucy Dobson of England was to receive 50 shares of refinery stock. Ten shares were left to each of Doyle's childen, ten to Dr. Haine, and ten to J. A. Hendren, the refinery clerk who was a pallbearer. Five shares went to each of the two children of Barney Gorman, who was employed by Gordon.

The Misses Charlotte and Jessie De Ro were to receive 50 shares each. Twenty-five shares were left to Doyle "to educate one of the children of Horace P. Janes," an attorney at one time associated with Doyle, who had died in 1862.

Additional legacies went to the Gordons' domestics. The Irish-born Annie Linnen and John Loughran, who were later married, were remembered, as were John T. Doyle's wife, George Boardman's wife, and Bernard Callahan, the chief engineer at the refinery. Sarah Foster, Gordon's sister, included in the original will, had pre-deceased him.

A final codicil made on May 21, 1869, as Gordon lay dying, reflected his bitterness at his daughter's marriage. In it he revoked the provisions in favor of Nellie. He bequeathed "the whole residue of his estate to his said wife, Elizabeth Ann Gordon," a death-bed action which clearly controverts the legend of his hatred for his wife.

Mrs. Gordon was also named an executor and had the choice of naming the other executors from a list drawn by Gordon. The list included John T. Doyle, Charles De Ro, John Redington, John H. Saunders, who was San Francisco City and County attorney, and Henry Williams, an attorney and city Commissioner of Deeds.

Mrs. Gordon did not select the executors at once, and on June 15 Doyle wrote urging her to make the selection immediately. Finally, she chose Doyle himself and John Redington, a prominent businessman who had been a neighbor of Gordon's in South Park.

Shortly after Gordon's death, various claims were presented to the executors of the estate. One of the first was that of banker John Parrott. On May 15, 1868, Gordon had borrowed from him $10,000 with interest at one percent per month. The following November, $5,000 had been paid plus the interest. The creditor's claim was for the balance, $5,393.33, in gold coin.

There were three claims from Glasgow, recalling the Gordons' European tour. A representative of the Walkinshaw Foundry, asserted that Gordon had ordered certain machinery, the cost of which was 422 pounds, 5 shillings. Another claim was presented by two "engineers and millwrights" doing business under the name of "The Patent Frictional Gearing Company." It was for 155 pounds, one shilling. They appointed as their agent Charles Forbes of San Francisco, a resident of South Park. A third claim from Glasgow was from William Wallace of The Chemical Laboratory, who sued for 686 pounds. He was represented in San Francisco by Laurence Kilgour, a broker associated with Horace Hill.

There were various claims filed by the Sugar Refinery against the Gordon estate. These were settled on December 20, 1870, with the payment of $16,746 to the refinery. Still another claim was presented by George Platt, in behalf of William T. Coleman, a resident of New York at that time. This suit reflects the ill-fated business association of Coleman and Gordon. Coleman sued Gordon's estate for $7,750, plus interest for four years, amounting to $2,447.

In September 1869, Doyle's firm petitioned Judge L. Archer of Santa Clara for payment of $1,000 monthly to Mrs. Gordon, pending settlement of the estate. The probate court was also informed that Thomas B. Bishop, the well known lawyer and land owner had been appointed referee to examine the accounts of the executors. The appraisers, appointed by the executors, were Faxon Atherton, George H. Howard and Tiburcio Parrott. Their report, dated July 8, 1878, showed the value of the estate as follows:

Mayfield Grange, 565 acres	$50,000.00
Notes from De Ro, secured by Refinery stock	59,121.30
Cash deposited in the London and S.F. Bank	21,439.07
Separate property at Mayfield Grange, 133 acres, with house, stables, etc.	50,000.00
Shares in the Refinery and other advances	90,000.00
In all	$277,259.87

This appraisal indicated a marked decline in the value of the Sugar Refinery's stock. However, by 1872, the executors were able to report that the estate had received from the refinery $26,270 in dividends and that the stock, when sold, had brought $203,542.48 to the heirs.

Also, as predicted by Gordon when he reluctantly left England in 1867 before completing his business, his "English letters patent for invention in the Sugar Refinery process" were listed as "no value." Gordon had once been offered $10,000 for his patents, and in 1867 considered them to be worth $40,000.

However, Gordon's estate was very large for that time, a notable increase in wealth for the pioneer who twenty years previously had arrived in San Francisco with only a few thousand dollars worth of lumber.

HELEN MAE "NELLIE" GORDON
Daughter of the George Gordons,
and wife of Dr. C. C. Gordon.

DOCTOR CHARLES CALHOUN GORDON
Husband of Nellie Gordon.
Both portraits courtesy of
the California Historical Society.

15

Decline of the House of Gordon

Nellie and her husband had apparently settled down in her father's home, in spite of George Gordon's dislike of his son-in-law. After George Gordon's death, they resided with Mrs. Gordon at Mayfield Grange. In July 1869, Nellie wrote asking for transfer of two hundred shares of the refinery's stock, informing the executors that the stock was hers and not part of her father's estate. The petition was signed by both Nellie and her husband.

Claims continued to harass the estate. Even the Limantour case of the 1850s appeared again when Northam and Whitmore, who aided in defeating the Limantour fraud, brought suit claiming George Gordon owed them $4,047 plus interest of $4,317.

On December 3, 1870, Mrs. Gordon wrote a lengthy letter to Doyle in which she discussed her financial affairs. She explained that she had signed claims sent to her which included one of Henry Sherwell of Nottingham, England, for work done for George Gordon while he was in England, and another from Kohler and Chase for a piano. Mrs. Gordon complained to Doyle that her income had been reduced and she had need of his financial aid.

The 1870 census of Santa Clara county reveals Mrs. Gordon listed the value of her real estate at $130,000 and her personal funds at $150,000. Her household included a Chinese cook and four servants, the latter all natives of Ireland. Dr. Charles C. Gordon is recorded as 32 years old and having assets of $13,000. His occupation is given as "none" but he apparently maintained an office and rooms in San Francisco, since the San Francisco Directory of 1870 still lists his office at Geary and Kearny, and his residence as the Occidental Hotel, while the 1871 directory lists a residence only, the Grand Hotel.

In 1870 a child was born to the young Gordons. On September 2, 1870, the newspapers reported that a son had been born at "Mayfield Grange, Menlo Park, to the wife of Dr. C. C. Gordon." This child was baptized at Trinity Episcopal Church on January 11, 1871, receiving the name of George A. Gordon. The records list the godparents as John J. Clarke, Mrs. Gordon's brother, and Adamina Cummings, George Gordon's sister, both residents of England. Shortly afterward, the child died.

The Gordons still appeared socially. In newspaper reports of the wedding of Alejandra Atherton to Major Lawrence Rathbone in February 1871, Nellie's dress was described, in accordance with the custom of that period. Later, an article of May 21, 1871, titled "Going Home Saturday Afternoon on the San Jose Railroad, Who Gets Out and Who Meets Them," the *Chronicle* included Dr. Gordon and Nellie. "Scores of our fashionables," this article noted, "are aboard going down to place themselves safely in the bosoms of their families until Monday morning calls them again to take into consideration the best means of amassing the almighty dollar, without which country seats cannot be kept up, with all their attendant expense." The writer described the well known owners of the estates in order of their disembarkation. The first stop was at the Seventeen Mile House, where D. O. Mills left the train; at the next stop, Oak Grove, John Redington and Alfred Poett departed; and at San Mateo, George Howard, John Parrott and François L. A. Pioche. Leaving the train at Fair Oaks were San Francisco's mayor Thomas Selby, Faxon Atherton and Milton Latham, while at Menlo Park, the departures of William Barron, John Doyle, and George Boardman are reported. At this station, Menlo Park, "The Gordon carriage now shows itself; it is here to meet the small man in grey who married George Gordon's heiress. In the carriage sits madam, who was once a beauty, and still retains some of her good looks."

During this period, various subdivisions in the Menlo Park area near the Gordon estate were advertised for sale. In 1868 the "Menlo Park Villa Extension" of 800 acres to its north was advertised. The next year the "Menlo Park Tract" of 630 acres adjacent to "Mayfield Grange, the residence and farm of George Gordon," was for sale. In March 1870 a new notice advertised "Villa Lots" at Menlo Park, "surrounded by the residences of Messrs. Selby, Atherton, Gordon, Barron, Woodworth, Castle, Meyer, Reis, Merrill, Otis, etc."

It is not surprising that Mrs. Gordon was offered a substantial amount for Mayfield Grange, and that she was interested to at least some extent. Faxon Atherton wrote his son, Faxon Jr., on March 16, 1872: "Mrs. Gordon is about to sell her house," and on April 12, "Mrs. Gordon was offered $85,000 for her place but deferred answering so long that the person who made it finally altered his mind. . . I am afraid she will never get such an offer again."

On March 20, 1872, G. W. Gordon, Dr. Gordon's attorney brother, wrote John T. Doyle, "The Ranch seems to me dirt cheap at $100,000 and in that sense I think the sale at $85,000 a great sacrifice."

Attorney Gordon's letter also refers to the presence of John J. Clark at Mayfield Grange. He had arrived a year earlier, although not since 1867 had he appeared in the directory of Lincoln, his former place of residence in England.

An earlier letter is of interest because it perhaps anticipates the future. Dr. Gordon wrote to Doyle on May 4, 1871, "I informed Mr. S. on Sunday I would let him know on what terms we would sell – as he wishes the whole ranch." Was "Mr. S" Leland Stanford? If so, it was several years before he finally obtained Mayfield Grange in 1876. It is of particular interest that Dr. Gordon's handwriting in this letter was most unsteady.

The distribution of George Gordon's estate proceeded slowly. On April 24, 1871, Nellie and her husband signed a document acknowledging receipt of $10,000 from Mrs. Gordon and John Redington. The next month Doyle, representing the children of H. P. Janes, filed claims. But still the settlements dragged on. In 1872 Hall and Cutler McAllister, representing several of the legatees, wrote to Doyle protesting the delays in the distribution.

In 1871, after the death of their child, Dr. and Mrs. Gordon made an extended tour of the East Coast. A letter from Dr. Gordon's attorney brother indicates that they were still out of the state in March 1872. Nellie returned alone that August according to railroad passenger records. It was probably at this time that the Gordons separated. Dr. Gordon is no longer listed in the San Francisco directories after 1872. They remained separated until Nellie's death less than two years later.

On April 4, 1874, Nellie Gordon died. The newspapers reported the death at Menlo Park of "Helen M., wife of C. C. Gordon, aged 29. Funeral at Trinity Church." She was buried at Laurel Hill. The cemetery records give the cause of death as "typhoid fever." The death certificate is signed by the same Dr. Haine who attended her father in his last illness.

In contrast to the later lurid accounts, Nellie's death as recorded was quite prosaic. There is no contemporary newspaper account of any unusual aspect, and Dr. Haine twice revealed intimate details of the alcoholism of Mrs. Gordon and her brother, while testifying in court, but made no reference to Nellie. It should be remembered that early deaths were not uncommon at that time.

Records of the Probate Court disclose Nellie's estate. She had considerable jewelry, the most valuable being two diamond rings worth $250.00. John Clark was listed as next of kin, John Redington as executor. Dr. Gordon was not mentioned, nor was her mother, who herself died three months after Nellie's death. The *San Mateo County Gazette* of Redwood City on July 11, 1874, announced that George Gordon's widow had died July 3 at "Menlo Park . . . a native of England, aged 49." Similar notices, all quite brief, were published in the San Francisco papers.

Like her husband and daughter, Mrs. Gordon was buried at Laurel Hill Cemetery. The records reveal the cause of death as "chronic hepatitis," i.e. chronic inflammation of the liver. This is a condition that is often the result of alcoholism, and helps confirm the legend of Mrs. Gordon's alcoholism. Her physician was the same Dr. Haine.

Mrs. Gordon had written her will on December 6, 1871. She left $500 to her cousin Elizabeth Eve in England. She bequeathed to John Doyle funds to aid in the erection of a "Roman Catholic Church in Menlo Park." Her brother John Clark was to receive one half of the residue of the estate, while her daughter was to receive the other half in a trust, and all her jewelry, silver and household goods. Faxon Atherton and John Redington were appointed trustees for Nellie's inheritance "free from control of any husband she may have or take." At her daughter's death, the trust was to be distributed to her issue, share and share alike if more than one issue, and if there was no issue at the time of her death "the estate to go to my right heirs." Lastly, Mrs. Gordon charged her daughter and her brother with "the duty of always maintaining the grave and burial lot wherein are interned the remains of my late husband, in proper order and repair." Doyle and her brother were named executors. The will suggests that she distrusted Nellie's husband and held continuing affection for George Gordon.

Then, in a codicil dated April 30, 1874, shortly after her daughter's death, Mrs. Gordon left almost all of her estate to her brother John Clark.

Two suits developed against her estate, both of interest. On August 13, 1874, the San Jose newspapers reported a "supplemental codicil, a letter dated June 23, 1874, written by the testatrix to a family servant, while the testatrix was in her last illness." The document is short. "Dear Old Nance: wish to give you my watch, two shawls and five thousand dollars. Your old friend E. A. Gordon."

Another newspaper article reported a "curious circumstance." There had been a servant in the family whose name was Nance, but Mrs. Gordon had a habit of calling "most everybody she liked 'dear Old Nance'." The article asserted that the "Dear Old Nance" referred to in the document was not a servant but a very interesting young lady of a totally dissimilar name, an acquaintance of Mrs. Gordon.

John Clark contested this codicil and the family of the "very interesting young lady" took it to court. The testimony is revealing. The "dear Old Nance" was indeed not a servant or nurse, but the daughter of the very social Gordon family friends, the Leander Ransomes! Matilda Ann Ransome, known as Annie, was the younger sister of Amelia Ransome Neville, who compiled a series of wonderful scrapbooks now located at the library of the California Historical Society. In them are many clippings regarding the "Old Nance" case; but neither in her book of reminiscences *Fantastic City,* nor in her scrapbooks is there any indication of her family's connection with the disputed codicil. Strangely, no newspaper identified the claimant as a daughter of the Leander Ransomes.

According to the testimony in the estate case, the Ransomes knew the Gordons in New York before they came to California and had been intimate friends the last six or seven years. This testimony is true, as the newspapers often reported the families attending the same social affairs. Also a letter at the California Historical Society from Mrs. Gordon to Mrs. Neville dated July 26, 1868, is further indication of the friendship. She wrote, "We are going to have the young girls of the neighborhood to a little dance [and] would be most happy to see you as we would Miss Anna." "It is not a party," explained Mrs. Gordon; "you need not bring a ball dress, merely a white something." She also asked Mrs. Neville to "bring Miss Annie's music with you."

In the trial Mrs. Ransome herself related how she

and her daughter Annie had arrived at Mayfield Grange on June 23, 1874, when Mrs. Gordon, whom she referred to as "Betsy," was on "her death bed." She claimed Mrs. Gordon had said: "Betsy's time is nearly over, I must be soon with G.G.," and on their leaving again repeated that she would "be soon with G.G." Mrs. Ransome further said that Mrs. Gordon often called her daughter Annie "Old Nance" or "Old Nancy," and that Mrs. Gordon insisted on writing the note leaving $5,000 to Annie. Interestingly, it was written when her brother, John Clark, was not in the room. Mrs. Gordon's health was sufficiently better to enable her to write the document.

Mrs. Doyle and her mother, Mrs. Pons, had driven over in their carriage that same day and they testified that during their visit Mrs. Gordon's health was better.

John T. Doyle also testified, stating Mrs. Gordon's health during her last illness was such that influence might have been exerted over her, but that he knew of "no aberration of her mind."

Mrs. Gordon's physician, Dr. Haine, also testified. He said Mrs. Gordon "very often took hot wine more or less diluted with water;" that she may have taken brandy and she had a habit of taking too much. Dr. Haine further related that she was so much in the habit of having port wine that she could not do without it.

Dr. Haine described John James Clark's conduct. He stated Clark never left the estate, as he was always intoxicated and not able to leave. He claimed Mrs. Gordon worried about the bills as Clark had power of attorney but was not paying them.

Dr. Haine also testified that when he remarked during Mrs. Gordon's last illness that "Clark would soon be the sole owner of this estate," Clark danced with delight. Clark's offensive reaction to Dr. Haine's announcement that his sister would soon die is somewhat similar to Mrs. Atherton's description of his action, described in the *Randolphs of Redwood* on learning of his sister's demise. This testimony substantiates the alcoholism of Mrs. Gordon as well as her brother.

The second suit was that of Dr. Joseph Haine (the same Jean Joseph Francois Haine who had attended George Gordon, his wife and Nellie) against John James Clark and John T. Doyle as executors of Mrs. Gordon's estate. Dr. Haine claimed he was owed $1,400, representing fourteen visits to Mayfield Grange between June 17, 1874, and Mrs. Gordon's death on July 3, of the same year. Examinations, advice and medicine had been given. The executors rejected his bill, being of the opinion that $100 per visit was too high.

Testifying for Dr. Haine were five well respected San Francisco physicians, Dr. Robert Mackintosh, Dr. Pigne Dupuytren, Dr. James C. Shorb, Dr. Benjamin D. Dean and Dr. Robert K. Nuttall. Testifying for the defendants, Doyle and Clark, were two equally respected medical men, Dr. J. D. Stillman and Dr. Henry Gibbons Jr. The testimony of the five prevailed and the court ordered Dr. Haine's bill to be paid in full. The *San Mateo County Gazette* criticized this high fee on March 20, 1875 under the caption "Deliver Me From My Physicians!"

While Clark was drinking a great deal, he also followed the advice of John T. Doyle and on October 17, 1874, authorized the attorney to be co-executor of the estate. On January 22, 1876, Clark notified the probate court that he was "in ill health" and resigned as administrator. Clark's signature in 1874 was not too firm, but in 1876 it was very shaky, hardly legible.

A month after his resignation, on February 4, 1876, John James Clark died. He was buried in the Gordon plot at Laurel Hill in San Francisco. The records state he was 46 years old (actually he was 47½ years old), a native of England, and that the cause of death was "phthisis" (i.e. tuberculosis). His heir was a former maid in the Gordon household.

The San Jose *Patriot* of February 28, 1876, gives a succinct account of the decline of the House of Gordon:

"John James Clark was left $300,000.00 by Mrs. Gordon on July 3, 1874. He had been of dissolute habits for some years and seemingly entered upon the enjoyment of his fortune with a determination to continue the life of an inebriate. Soon the unequal contest with King Alcohol began to tell upon the health of the legatee and in six months he learned he was not long for this world. About this time he conceived a fancy for a Miss Wallace, who had been an inmate of Mr. Gordon's house in the capacity of a dressing maid, and married her. His health continued to fail and he died about two months since, leaving his entire estate to his wife. The former servant is in luck!"

"Miss Wallace" was Margaret Teresa Wallace, a native of Ireland. In leaving his estate to his wife, Clark stated he had no "father or mother, brother or sister or any descendants surviving him." The probate was commenced on February 7, 1876, and closed October 27, 1877. Clark's estate was appraised at $131,000, the major asset being "Mayfield Grange." He had been leasing out the farmland, much of it to Michael Keefe of San Mateo County who raised hay and grain and had the right to use the field for grazing after the crops were harvested. The estate also included two promissory notes, one of Horatio P. Livermore for $17,000, one of William M. Moore for $5000.

Mayfield Grange had been appraised at $100,000 in Clark's estate, but in 1876 Mrs. Clark sold it for $170,000 to Leland Stanford. She returned to Ireland to visit her parents, and there she died on December 25, 1878, in Michelstown, County Cork. Her will was probated in California, and a number of Catholic organizations in that state shared with her relatives the fruits of George Gordon's labors.

On January 28, 1879, John T. Doyle and John H. Redington filed a copy of her will and were appointed executors. The estate was valued at $125,000, considerably less than the amount Stanford had paid for Mayfield Grange just three years previously. Father Dennis M. Dempsey, who had been pastor of St. Dennis' Church in Menlo Park, was left $500, as was Father William Bowman, a one-time pastor of St. Matthew's, San Mateo. Archbishop Alemany of San Francisco received $14,000 to be distributed as follows: $5,000 to the Roman Catholic Orphan Asylum, $2,000 to the Sisters of Mercy, $5,000 for the boys' orphanage at San Rafael (St. Vincent's) and $2,000 to the Reverend Mother May Joseph (O'Rourke) for the hospital under her care, St. Mary's on Bryant Street.

Margaret Teresa Clark also left $5,000 to her parents, John and Mary Wallace (her father died before the estate was settled), and the same in trust for her brother Daniel Wallace. Her sister Kate Josephine Powell of County Cork received her jewelry, wearing apparel and $30,000 in trust; her sister Mary Little of Brooklyn and her brother Richard Wallace of Cork received $10,000 each. The residue was left in trust for a nephew, Joseph Sedgwick of Portland, Oregon.

One of Mrs. Clark's brothers, Daniel Wallace of San Francisco, dissatisfied with his $5,000 trust, retained the well known, flamboyant attorney General William H. L. Barnes to attempt to revoke his sister's will. Wallace claimed "undue influence and fraudulent misrepresentation." His sister, he stated, "was not of sound mind, but was non compos mentis." General Barnes added during the trial that Mrs. Clark "at the time of signing the will and a long time subsequent, and in fact down to the day of her death . . . had never drawn a sober breath."

Not all of Gordon's Irish-born servants were alcoholics. The Loughrans left Mayfield Grange shortly after Gordon's death, invested in real estate, and established a home in Menlo Park. After Loughran's 1886 death, the *Times-Gazette* described him as "distinguished by generous hospitality and kindly deeds."

The court ruled, on December 29, 1878, against the petitioner, Daniel Wallace, and the will remained as drawn.

Shortly after this, the missing Dr. Gordon reentered into the story. The executors of Mrs. Clark's will sued the National Gold Bank of San Francisco and Dr. Charles C. Gordon in the Superior Court of California in San Francisco. They were suing for possession of a sealed trunk marked "Dr. C.C.G." containing "a certain lot of silver" valued at $1,500 which they claimed belonged to the estate of Margaret Teresa Clark. In the court proceedings, attorney Robert L. Behre swore that on February 16, 1880 he "posted a summons to C. C. Gordon at his place of residence, Trinidad, Territory of Colorado." According to a recent book, *Hippocrates in a Red Vest* by Barron Beshoar, Dr. Gordon was a medical associate of the "frontier doctor" Michael

Beshoar. Trinidad at this time, was a wild western town, where the doctors carried Colt revolvers, a decided change for the former squire of Mayfield Grange! Dr. Gordon's stay in Trinidad was not lengthy as he moved south to Fort Union where he served as an army doctor, then in 1882 went to Las Vegas, New Mexico. There he became city physician, apparently distinguishing himself during the smallpox epidemic of 1882-1883. In 1889 the city's newspaper, the *Optic,* noted: "Dr. Gordon is doing good work for the people of Las Vegas and no man would be missed more than he, should the town lose him." It did not until many years later. According to historian S. Omar Barker, he died in Las Vegas on April 21, 1923 – almost fifty years after the deaths of the California Gordons. This is a Dr. Gordon quite at variance to Gertrude Atherton's description of him as a "miserable specimen of a man," or to the statement of Robert O'Brien and others that he was "an alcoholic, who drank himself to death" about the time Nellie died.

One might speculate as to whether or not the contents of the small trunk were part of the auction held in the fall of 1882 that was referred to by Mrs. Atherton in her novels. There had been an earlier sale of some of Nellie's possessions through the Probate Court on September 21, 1877, when certain of her silverware such as vases, spoons, a card receiver, etc. were sold to John Redington for $344.45.

In 1886 Doyle filed the final suit in the matter of the George Gordon estate in the Santa Clara County Superior Court. He stated that the "San Francisco Sugar Refining Company, subsequently the San Francisco and Pacific Sugar Company," which imported raw sugar "from Manila and elsewhere" paid higher

insurance premiums on its maritime policies during the
Civil War because of the raids of the *Alabama* and
other Confederate vessels "equipped and armed in English ports." After the war an international tribunal
awarded the United States $15,500,000 from England
for the loss of ships, cargoes and for increased insurance
rates. Doyle admitted he was not well acquainted with
the refinery's business but he asked that, since George
Gordon was the principal stockholder in the company,
the money received by the refinery from the "Geneva
award fund" be refunded to the estate.

Also partners to this suit were George M. Pinney Jr.
of New York, James L. King of San Francisco, and
Barling and Beaman of New York, who had been
clerks at the now defunct William T. Coleman and
Company of New York when Coleman had been repre-
senting the refinery.

The final settlement, approved by the court, was that,
since there were no Gordon heirs alive, the bills of
Doyle and the others involved in obtaining the money
from the Alabama claim settlement would be paid from
the sum received in the following proportions: 25% to
Pinney and King, 20% to Barling and Beaman, and the
remaining 55% to Doyle. By what could hardly have
been coincidence, the bills rendered by these gentlemen
had amounted to the exact sum of the money received.
Thus ended the last of the many law suits in which
George Gordon was a principal, the attorneys being the
main beneficiaries!

At the time of Gordon's death, his refinery was still
the leading producer of sugar on the Pacific coast and
claimed to be the "largest sugar refining establishment
in the United States." Charles De Ro had become president after Gordon's resignation was accepted on May

20, 1869. Doyle had earlier written Ralston giving his opinion that De Ro had knowledge of the sugar business. He had been successful as an auctioneer and a trustee of the refinery.

Although 1869 was a good year for the refinery with profits totaling $59,296.05, the business appears to have gradually decreased in the years following. De Ro remained as president until his death in 1873 at the age of 45. By 1874, Claus Spreckels' California Sugar Refinery was claiming to be the largest sugar refining firm in California. The man whom Gordon a few years before had referred to as "that fool, Spreckles" [*sic*] was well on his way to becoming the Pacific Coast "Sugar King."

John S. Hittell, in his *Commerce and Industries of the Pacific Coast* published in 1882, reported that Gordon's San Francisco refinery, then owned by D. O. Mills, N. Luning and W. T. Coleman, was closed. This property at 8th and Harrison, however, long continued to be recorded in the name of the San Francisco and Pacific Sugar Refinery. It is now the location of a car and truck rental company.

Meanwhile, because Gordon's efforts to establish a beet sugar industry in California had been curtailed by his illness and death, the honor of establishing the nation's first successful beet sugar refinery went to Ebenezer Herrick Dyer. His company was organized the year of George Gordon's death and began operations three years later at Alvarado on the south shore of San Francisco Bay.

Gordon's pioneer enterprise, the first successful sugar refinery in California, declined and faded away after his death. His business, like his family, appeared to need the energy of the dynamic George Gordon.

16

Epilogue

The obituaries of George Gordon were, as noted, most laudatory, and through a number of succeeding years, he continued to be praised in print. In 1870, Benjamin P. Avery, an editor of the famous *Overland Monthly* and later United States minister to China, prepared a sketch of Gordon for Oscar T. Shuck's *Representative and Leading Men of the Pacific.* "He was a man of great practical sagacity and enterprise," wrote Avery, "and joined to an original mind, strengthened by varied culture and observation, much public spirit and energy of will."

In the Special Collections section of the library of the University of California at Los Angeles there is an 1872 pamphlet which demonstrates the respect with which Gordon's writings were held, even after his death in 1869. The pamphlet is entitled, "Mortgage Tax Question, 1871: An Address to the Legislature of California." Its author wrote: "I append to these remarks a letter from a gentleman of well-known ability, now deceased, which contains some apt practical illustrations of the subject matter." The appended letter, signed by Gordon, is dated South Park, February 6, 1859, and addressed to "The Tenth Legislature of California which met in 1859, and especially the Honorable M. Kirkpatrick of the Senate," a member from Sierra County. The letter was headed: "Shall money and mortgages be taxed? To those who borrow or expect to borrow – to traders or such as expect to trade – to real estate owners or those that hope to own some." In the lengthy discussion which followed, Gordon expressed his views on taxation, and included the statement that taxes are "absurdly unequal." As an example, he mentioned the poll tax, which taxes a "millionaire and a pauper" equally. His comments were still pertinent.

In 1884 the *Bulletin* of August 25, in an article regarding the fate of Gordon's estate, added, "It would hardly be exaggeration to say that from the day of his arrival continuously to that of his death, compassing a period of just twenty years, he was among the foremost of our citizens for public spirit and business energy, enterprise and sagacity. His mind, so practical, was yet not dry. It was Baconian."

Many ambitious, adventurous Argonauts did, like Gordon, find in California wealth and prominence. Gordon did more; he entered into controversies affecting the public good, expressing himself regardless of the consequences. While his position on the Bulkhead question was a popular one, his opposition to the second Committee of Vigilance was most unpopular. Just before the Civil War, when passions in both the North and the South were high, Gordon made a plea for peace, stating it in calm, logical terms. Gordon's views, examined with the advantageous perspective of time, were usually correct; many, like his ideas on earthquake-proof building construction and beet sugar refining, were later proved sound.

While many of Gordon's contemporaries were mere money-makers, Gordon himself was more. He stood aside from a number of the business involvements of his time. The mining stock mania which was so widespread in San Francisco in the 1860s did not affect him; his name does not appear as an officer or stockholder in any of the hundreds of mining companies formed in that decade. Nor does his name appear in the lists of directors of the numerous San Francisco insurance companies which included most of the prominent businessmen of the period. Nor was it included in the membership rolls of such fashionable clubs as the Union, or the prestigious Society of California Pioneers. Considering Gordon's wealth, his civic activities, his popular hospitality, it has been justifiably said that "he did not take the rank in the community which he should have." Just why that is so remains a matter for conjecture.

John T. Doyle had a very important role as a stabilizing factor and a confidant in Gordon's life and in that of his heirs, including the Clarks. During the decline of the family, it was from Doyle that the alcoholic legatees sought advice. In his recollections of George Gordon written in 1902, Doyle characterized him as a "remarkably bright and clever man, at home on all mechanical questions and possessed of very considerable knowledge of different branches of natural science." Yet as intimate as Doyle was with Gordon, his recollections reveal no accurate knowledge of Gordon's life before he arrived in California.

Another contemporary, the family friend Amelia Ransome Neville, characterized the Gordons: "Mrs. Gordon and pretty Miss Nellie were conspicuous in the social scene and George Gordon himself was just generally conspicuous. He had that British sense of a gentleman's duty to offer constructive criticism of public affairs which inspires so many letters to the London 'Times,' and was forever rushing into print about something."

To return to the Gordon legend, it is clear that much of it was untrue. An example, typical of numerous allegations without basis, is the claim that Mrs. Gordon laced her infant daughter's milk with whiskey. That there was alcoholism in the family has been shown to be a fact. However, this appears to have been accentuated after George Gordon's death and especially during the period when the Clarks were the masters of Mayfield Grange. The marked decline of the Gordon estate under the aegis of the Clarks possibly created a darker portraiture of Nellie and Mrs. Gordon than was justified.

Marcus Boruck in his *Illustrated Spirit of the Times* wrote only a year after the last Gordon heir had left Mayfield Grange: "There is a tinge of romance in the former history and rather a sad story as we heard it related. . . [Gordon] sickened and died and afterwards there was an apparent fatality attending the place he had cherished with so much care. As the years rolled on, it fell into neglect and there were strange stories, which it is needless to rehearse, of the people who lived there. The flowers and shrubbery were choked with weeds, the house was becoming dilapidated and the ownership lapsed to those who had no eye for beauty."

That George Gordon had a great love for his daughter is shown in the surviving letters and by his actions. His reaction to his daughter's marriage is one many fathers have had. As Nellie's marriage had a duration of only two years, possibly her father's opposition was warranted.

Gordon's affection for his new country, America, was amply illustrated in his life, although he never became a citizen. In his 1859 article, "Mining Titles," he explained: "Anything of reason and truth in this letter may be disparaged, because the writer is not technically a citizen of the United States. In mere form your correspondent is not – unfinished private business prevents him. In substance he is, as you know, one of the early pioneers of California, intimately connected with its industrial pursuits, literally without an interest or almost a connection outside of the State, he would hardly be a more inveterate Californian were he native born. He who loves Athens is an Athenian."

Why did he not become a citizen? Was he fearful that his true surname of Cummings would be revealed? Was there sufficient advantage in remaining an alien so that he could have his many litigations assigned to the federal rather than state courts? These and other questions remain unanswered.

Details of his life in England, the reason for the change in his name, particulars of his life on the eastern seaboard remain in part unknown. Only after the discovery of gold in California does Gordon's career become well documented.

The Gordon family has long since disappeared, as has the source of its wealth, the Sugar Refinery. In fact, George Gordon's name remains firmly attached to only one place in San Francisco, a short lane off Harrison Street near Ninth called "Gordon." Yet this self-styled "inveterate Californian" is well remembered as the creator of South Park, and perhaps this volume will in some measure give him a just place in history as a constructive resident who contributed much to his adopted city and state.

Index